THE PERSIAN STORM

BIBLICAL PROPHECY AND IRAN'S LASTING THREAT TO ISRAEL

MARK HITCHCOCK

NELSON BOOKS
An Imprint of Thomas Nelson

The Persian Storm

Published in Nashville, Tennessee, by Nelson Books, an imprint of Thomas Nelson, 501 Nelson Place, Nashville, TN 37214, USA. Nelson Books and Thomas Nelson are registered trademarks of HarperCollins Christian Publishing, Inc.

Thomas Nelson titles may be purchased in bulk for educational, business, fund-raising, or sales promotional use. For information, please email SpecialMarkets@ThomasNelson.com.

ISBN 978-1-4003-5632-4 (ePub)
ISBN 978-1-4003-5631-7 (TP)

HarperCollins Publishers, Macken House, 39/40 Mayor Street Upper, Dublin 1, D01 C9W8, Ireland (https://www.harpercollins.com).

Library of Congress Cataloging-in-Publication Data on File

9781400356317

Printed in the United States of America

26 27 28 29 30 LBC 5 4 3 2 1

To my daughter-in-law Ellen
You're a wonderful blessing from God to
Samuel and your precious children,
but also to me and our entire family beyond
anything we could ask or think.
I thank God every day for making
you part of our family
and bringing your radiant joy into our lives.

CONTENTS

AN URGENT NOTE: IRAN IN TURMOIL

AS I WRITE THESE WORDS, Iran once again dominates the headlines, with massive ongoing military strikes on the country by American and Israeli forces.

This follows a protest movement among Iran's people that began on December 28, 2025, reflecting popular discontent over a collapsed currency and soaring inflation. The Iranian rial had lost nearly 80 percent of its value, and ordinary Iranians could no longer afford basic necessities.

What started with shopkeepers and merchants in Tehran's Grand Bazaar soon spread to all thirty-one provinces of the nation. Millions poured into the streets, becoming what many were calling the largest popular uprising in Iran since the 1979 Islamic Revolution.

The headlines that followed were staggering and heartbreaking:

Iran International reported that by January 10, 2026, at least two thousand protesters had been killed nationwide over the previous forty-eight hours as Iranian security forces escalated their use of live ammunition against demonstrators. Hospitals in Tehran and Shiraz became overwhelmed with injured protesters, many suffering gunshot wounds.[1] (More recent estimates have been counting the number of dead as between thirty and forty thousand.) On January 3, when security forces killed at least eleven protesters, Supreme Leader Ali Khamenei—who would later be killed in the American-Israeli strikes that began on February 28—declared that "rioters should be put in their place."[2]

CNN reported that protesters described "enormous crowds and feelings of hope, but also brutal violence and 'bodies piled up on each other' in a hospital." A doctor told CNN that hospitals were "extremely chaotic" and patients were terrified to be identified amid the crackdown by authorities.[3]

The Iranian government imposed a near-total internet blackout after January 8 in an attempt to hide the scale of both the protests and the violent crackdown. Despite this communications shutdown, footage continued to emerge of protesters chanting "Death to the Dictator" and "Death to Khamenei"—slogans that once would have meant certain execution. Some even shouted "Long live the Shah," expressing support for the return of Reza Pahlavi, the exiled son of the last Shah who fled Iran in 1979.[4]

U.S. President Donald Trump repeatedly threatened military action against Iran if the regime continued killing protesters. According to Iran International, Trump received a briefing from senior officials on January 12 on possible responses, "including military strikes, cyber operations, and psychological measures to support protesters." Meanwhile, Iranian Foreign Minister Abbas Araghchi stated that Iran was open to negotiations but also "fully prepared for war."[5]

As negotiations dragged on, the Americans and Israelis lost patience with the lack of perceived progress. Their threatened military punishment became a crushing reality.

No one knows how this will ultimately end. Will some remnant version of the Islamic Republic survive? Will there be civil war? Foreign intervention? A negotiated transition? The situation changes rapidly.

A BOOK ABOUT THE BIBLE, NOT THE HEADLINES

This book was written during one of the most volatile periods in Middle Eastern history. In the time since I began working on this manuscript, we have witnessed the October 7, 2023, Hamas attack on Israel and the devastating war that followed; Israel's assassination of Hezbollah leader Hassan Nasrallah in September 2024; the stunning collapse of Syria's Assad regime in December 2024 after fifty-four years of family rule; direct military confrontation between Israel and Iran in April and October 2024; Israel's massive Operation Rising Lion strikes against Iranian nuclear facilities in June 2025; American military strikes on Iran's most fortified nuclear sites; a twelve-day war followed by a fragile ceasefire; a popular uprising that may reshape Iran for the foreseeable future, and now, a massive military pounding from military forces of the U.S. and Israel that brought about the deaths of Supreme Leader Ali Khamenei and several other Iranian leaders.

I have done my best to update this book to reflect these seismic developments. But here is what I want you to understand: *By the time you hold this book in your hands, the situation will almost certainly look different than it does today.* The current turmoil in Iran may evolve in ways that none of us can now predicted.

But here is what I know with absolute certainty: However this crisis resolves, *God will take care of it.* He always does. The Lord is never caught off guard by the affairs of nations. He is never scrambling to adjust His plans. Whatever happens in Iran, whatever government rises or falls, whatever leaders emerge or disappear, God's prophetic purposes will march forward exactly as He has ordained.

This book is not ultimately about current events. It's about Bible prophecy. And the Word of God does not change with the headlines.

The prophet Ezekiel, writing more than 2,600 years ago, foretold that in the "latter years" a nation called Persia, which is modern-day Iran, would join a coalition of nations led by a ruler from the far north to invade Israel. This prophecy, found in chapters 38 and 39 of Ezekiel, has never been finally fulfilled. But the stage for that fulfillment is being set in remarkable ways, as I document throughout this book.

Here is something crucial to understand: Nowhere does Ezekiel specify what kind of government Persia will have when this invasion occurs. The prophecy does not say Iran will be ruled by ayatollahs or mullahs, or that Iran will be an Islamic theocracy, a democracy, or a restored monarchy. The Bible simply says that Persia, the geographic territory we know as Iran, will be part of this end-time coalition against Israel.

This means that regardless of what happens in the current uprising, whether the Islamic Republic survives, transforms, or collapses entirely, the prophetic trajectory remains unchanged. God's Word will be fulfilled. Iran, in whatever political form it takes, will ultimately play the role Ezekiel described.

PERSIA'S PLACE IN GOD'S STORY

It's worth pausing to remember that Persia has a long and significant history in God's unfolding plan. This is not the first time this ancient nation has stood at the center of world events and biblical history.

The prophet Daniel served in the courts of Persia and received some of the most detailed prophetic visions in all of Scripture while living under Persian rule. And in the prophecies of Isaiah, it was Persia's King Cyrus whom God called "my shepherd" and "his anointed" (Isaiah 44:28; 45:1)—remarkable titles for a pagan king! The fulfillment of this prophecy came when Cyrus later issued the decree allowing the Jewish exiles to return to Jerusalem and rebuild the Temple, as recorded in the books of Ezra and Nehemiah. The book of Esther takes place entirely in Persia, where God providentially preserved the Jewish people from annihilation through a plot that eerily foreshadows modern Iranian threats against Israel.

In other words, Persia has been part of God's story for millennia. The land we now call Iran has witnessed the rise and fall of empires, the preservation of God's people, and the unfolding of Bible prophecy. And according to Ezekiel, Persia's role in God's prophetic drama is not yet complete.

This perspective helps us understand why current events in Iran matter. But it also lets us see why they don't matter in the way we might think. The current regime, for all its bluster and violence, is just one chapter in a much longer story. Ayatollahs have ruled Iran for less than fifty years. The Persian civilization stretches back more than 2,500 years. And God's purposes for this land extend into eternity. Whatever government exists in Iran when Ezekiel 38 is fulfilled, it will be because God has orchestrated history to bring about His perfect plan. Persia will be there when Ezekiel's prophecies unfold, regardless of who rules in Tehran.

GOD IS ORCHESTRATING

As you read this book, you may find specific details I describe that have already changed. Governments shift.

Leaders fall. Alliances realign. But the prophetic framework remains rock solid.

One of the great themes of Bible prophecy is God's absolute sovereignty over the rise and fall of nations. In Ezekiel 38, God declares to the future leader of this invasion: "I will turn you about and put hooks into your jaws, and I will bring you out" (38:4). God Himself will draw these nations into this ill-fated invasion. He is orchestrating history according to His predetermined plan.

This truth should bring us great comfort in uncertain times. When we watch the chaos unfolding in Iran, when we see the violence and bloodshed and wonder where it's all headed, we can be sure that God is not surprised. He is not wringing His hands in heaven, wondering what will happen next. He is working all things "according to the counsel of His will" (Ephesians 1:11 ESV).

The psalmist declared: "Why do the nations rage and the peoples plot in vain? . . . He who sits in the heavens laughs; the Lord holds them in derision" (Psalm 2:1,4 ESV). Human rulers may scheme and plot, protesters may rise up, regimes may fall—but God remains on His throne.

Through the prophet Isaiah, God expresses it even more directly: "I am God, and there is no other; I am God, and there is none like me, declaring the end from the beginning and from ancient times things not yet done, saying, 'My counsel shall stand, and I will accomplish all my purpose'" (Isaiah 46:9–10). This is the God we serve. He declared what would happen to Persia in the latter days more than 2,600 years ago, and His counsel will stand.

Daniel 2:21 reminds us that God "removes kings and sets up kings." Whether Iran's current Supreme Leader remains in power or is swept away by this uprising, it will be because God has ordained it. This doesn't mean we shouldn't pray for justice or grieve over suffering. It means we can trust that God is working even through the chaos.

A HEART FOR THE IRANIAN PEOPLE

Before going further, I want to express something that weighs heavily on my heart: my deep concern and compassion for the Iranian people.

As I watch the footage emerging from Iran—of the protests, the violence, the killing of unarmed demonstrators, the internet blackout designed to hide atrocities—my heart breaks for the millions of ordinary Iranians caught in this crisis. These are mothers and fathers, sons and daughters, students and shopkeepers who simply want to feed their families and live in freedom. Many are risking everything, including their lives, to cry out for change.

Throughout this book, I speak critically of the Iranian regime led by Khamenei and the mullahs, a theocracy that has oppressed Iran's people and threatened Israel's destruction for more than four decades. But please understand: My criticism is directed at Iran's rulers, not its people. The Iranian people are not my enemies. They are precious souls created in the image of God, loved by Him, and in need of the same Savior we all need.

Indeed, one of the most remarkable spiritual developments of our time is the explosive growth of Christianity inside Iran. Despite severe persecution, or perhaps because of it, Iran is now home to one of the fastest-growing churches in the world. Some estimates suggest that more Iranians have come to faith in Christ in the past twenty-five years than in the previous thirteen centuries combined. Iranians are leaving Islam in record numbers and turning to Jesus Christ. House churches multiply even as the regime arrests and imprisons believers. The recent instability and the Iranian people's disillusionment with the regime have only accelerated this spiritual hunger. God is at work in Iran, not just geopolitically, but spiritually.

I have had the privilege of meeting Iranian believers who fled persecution and now live in the West. Their faith should inspire all of us. They understand what it means to count the cost of following Jesus. Their testimonies remind me that while we focus on the geopolitical significance of Iran, God's heart is for the Iranian people themselves.

As you read about Iran's role in end-time prophecy, please join me in praying for the Iranian people. Pray for their safety amid the current violence. Pray for the spread of the gospel. Pray that many Iranians would come to know Jesus Christ as Lord and Savior. And pray for the believers inside Iran who are risking their lives to share the good news. They are our brothers and sisters in Christ, and they need our prayers.

READING THIS BOOK IN UNCERTAIN TIMES

You may be wondering how you can trust what this book says when everything in Iran seems to be changing so fast.

Here's my answer: That's precisely why Bible prophecy matters.

Human predictions fail. Intelligence assessments prove wrong. Experts are constantly surprised by events they didn't see coming. Who predicted the sudden collapse of Assad's regime in Syria in December 2024? Who foresaw that protests over bread prices would erupt in 2026 into the largest uprising in Iran since 1979? The pundits are always playing catch-up with history.

But the same God who predicted the rise and fall of Babylon, Persia, Greece, and Rome, with pinpoint accuracy, centuries in advance, has also revealed the outline of end-time events. We may not know every detail. But we can trust the prophetic framework God gave us.

This book is about understanding the biblical template that makes sense of our world. It doesn't tell you exactly what will happen next week in Iran; rather, it shows how current events fit into the larger prophetic picture that culminates in the return of Jesus Christ.

Some people worry that studying Bible prophecy will make us numb to the tragedy we see in the world. But I've found the opposite to be true. When we understand that Jesus could return at any moment, it motivates us to live with urgency, to share the gospel boldly, and to invest our lives in things that matter for eternity. Prophecy is not meant to satisfy our curiosity about the future; God gave it to us to transform how we live in the present. As the apostle John wrote after describing the return of Christ: "Everyone who has this hope in him purifies himself, just as he is pure" (1 John 3:3 NIV).

The events unfolding in Iran today—as dramatic and significant as they are—are just one small part of that larger story. All of history is moving toward the fulfillment of God's prophetic Word. That should give us peace and confidence.

Whether you're reading this while Iran still burns, or months or years later when the current crisis is a distant memory, the message remains the same:

God is in control. His Word is true. And Jesus is coming.

MARK HITCHCOCK
Edmond, Oklahoma
March 2026

INTRODUCTION: BEYOND THE HEADLIGHTS

SEVERAL YEARS AGO I found myself driving down the interstate between Oklahoma City and Dallas in the worst rainstorm I've ever experienced. Darkness and driving rain descended like a heavy blanket. Traffic slowed to a crawl as drivers strained to see the road or anything in front of them. Everything was covered in a sheet of rain. All I could see was the hood of my car. Automobiles and trucks, trying to avoid slamming into each other, were pulling over and stopping beneath underpasses because they couldn't see even a few feet beyond the headlights in the relentless storm. Fortunately, I was among those able to find sanctuary to wait it out. Have you ever been there? Traveling down the road, straining and longing to see beyond the headlights, to see what's ahead. If only you could know what's coming next—could know or predict what lies just in front of you or just around the next bend in the road. Everywhere we look today our world appears more and more like a dark storm with a drenching downpour, especially when it comes to Israel and Iran and Iran's allies. The sky is black and threatening. In the dark, uncertain days of this gathering storm, we all long to see beyond the headlights—to know, to have some sense of where things are headed, and to calm our troubled hearts.

Is there a reliable source to show us what lies ahead? To shine through the darkness?

A SURE WORD

The biblical prophets of old claimed to know the future, including the final series of apocalyptic events that will bring this age to its stunning climax. By consulting their predictions, you and I can know the future of people and nations, because world events—including current events—are part of a larger story scripted ahead of time.

In recent years, many of these predictions have come to pass with sobering accuracy. Forecasts have become headlines. Prophetic possibilities have become geopolitical realities. Yet the larger prophetic picture—the ultimate showdown described by Ezekiel—still lies ahead. The pace of fulfillment has dramatically accelerated since 2023, with events moving at unprecedented speed. What once seemed like distant scenarios have materialized with startling clarity.

On October 7, 2023, Hamas launched a coordinated surprise attack on Israel, killing over 1,200 people and taking 251 hostages.[1] This assault triggered Israel's longest military conflict—a war that would fundamentally reshape the Middle East. Israel's response was swift and overwhelming, lasting more than two years and resulting in massive casualties on both sides.[2]

In September 2024, Israel assassinated Hassan Nasrallah, the longtime leader of Hezbollah, in a massive airstrike on Beirut.[3] This operation, along with extensive ground campaigns in Lebanon, severely degraded Iran's most powerful proxy force. Israel's precision strikes demonstrated an intelligence penetration of Iranian networks that shocked the region.

Then, in December 2024, came an event few had predicted: the sudden collapse of Syria's Assad regime after fifty-four years of family rule.[4] Within twelve days, rebel forces swept through Syria's major cities and captured Damascus, forcing Bashar al-Assad to flee to Russia. This stunning development severed Iran's critical land corridor to Hezbollah and dealt a strategic blow to Tehran's regional influence.

The showdown between Israel, the United States, and Iran escalated from shadow warfare to direct military confrontation in 2024. Iran launched over three hundred missiles and drones against Israel in April 2024, followed by approximately two hundred ballistic missiles in October.[5] Israel retaliated with strikes targeting Iranian air defenses and military installations. But these exchanges were merely a prelude.

In June 2025, Israel launched Operation Rising Lion—a massive surprise attack on Iran itself, striking nuclear facilities, military bases, and assassinating top Iranian commanders.[6] Days later, the United States joined the conflict, bombing Iran's most hardened, fortified nuclear sites.[7] After twelve days of intense fighting, a ceasefire was negotiated.[8] Yet everyone knows this is not the end—it's merely a pause in an unresolved conflict.

Most alarming, Iran's nuclear program has reached critical mass—as we'll review more closely in chapter 2. By mid-2025, Iran had stockpiled over 400 kilograms of uranium enriched to 60 percent purity—just below the 90 percent threshold needed for nuclear weapons.[9] According to the International Atomic Energy Agency (IAEA), this is enough fissile material for more than a dozen nuclear weapons if further enriched.[10] Intelligence assessments indicate Iran's "breakout time"—the period needed to enrich enough uranium for one nuclear weapon—has shrunk from twelve months to less than one week.[11] Some analysts say it's effectively zero.

In June 2025, the IAEA formally found Iran to be in breach of its nuclear safeguards obligations for the first time since 2005.[12] Israeli Prime Minister Benjamin Netanyahu stated that Iran could produce a nuclear weapon "in a very short time," citing this as the justification for Israel's preemptive strikes.[13]

Yet the larger prophetic picture—the ultimate showdown described by the prophet Ezekiel—still lies ahead. This makes the ancient prophecies more relevant, not less, as we watch the final pieces continue to fall into place. The alignment continues:

- Russia, Iran, and Turkey, a major part of the exact coalition described in Ezekiel 38, are working together in unprecedented ways, despite Syria's political transformation affecting their strategic calculations.
- Israel has moved from shadow operations to direct military strikes against Iran's nuclear program and military infrastructure.
- The network of Iranian proxies throughout the region has been significantly degraded but not eliminated.
- The international community has exhausted diplomatic options to constrain Iran's nuclear ambitions.

These developments are not random. Events in the Middle East continue to unfold just as we should expect if we consult the biblical end-time template. The buildup continues, though the timeline remains known only to God.

We don't have to follow the predictions of the biblical prophets blindly. We can put their prophecies to the test because hundreds of them have already been literally fulfilled with 100 percent accuracy. The Bible, which was 28 percent prophecy at the time it was written, is the only book in existence with a long, extensive track record of accurately predicting the future. The best estimates are that the Bible contains about one thousand prophecies. Up to now, five hundred of those have been literally, precisely fulfilled. With that performance history we can be sure that the Bible's unfulfilled prophecies will come to pass just as surely and literally as those that have already been fulfilled.

For this reason, through the centuries, people from all walks of life and backgrounds have turned again and again to the Bible's ancient end-time prophecies to discover God's plan for human history. By studying the ancient writings, we can know the pattern of events foretold by the prophets long ago and written in Scripture.

As we turn to the pages of Scripture today, we discover that as unsettling and alarming as current events are, they shouldn't surprise us in light of end-time prophecy. The crisis in Iran and the Middle East has continued to intensify exactly as Scripture predicted. In recent years we've witnessed:

- Iran's nuclear program advancing to the threshold of weapons capability, with enrichment levels and stockpiles far exceeding any peaceful purpose.
- Direct military confrontation between Israel and Iran, including large-scale strikes on Iranian territory.
- The ongoing alignment of Russia, Iran, and Turkey, which is the exact coalition described in Ezekiel 38.
- Dramatic shifts in Syria's political landscape, affecting Iran's strategic calculations.
- The weakening yet persistence of Iran's proxy network throughout the region.

THE PROPHETIC ALLIANCES TAKES SHAPE

The convergence of the three powers of Russia, Iran, and Turkey reached a remarkable milestone in October 2024 when Turkish President Erdoğan explicitly called for a Russia-Iran-Turkey alliance against Israel. Speaking to Turkish media, Erdoğan declared it was "essential that Russia, Iran and Syria take more effective measures" in response to Israeli actions.

This represents the first time in history that these specific nations have formed such an alliance. For over 2,600 years since Ezekiel wrote his prophecy, the nations he identified—Rosh (Russia), Persia (Iran), and Meschech, Tubal, Gomer, and Beth-Togarmah (Turkey)—had never aligned in this configuration. Throughout the Ottoman Empire, the Soviet era, and the Cold War, these powers were typically adversaries or, at best, neutral toward each other.

Today's alignment defies conventional geopolitical logic. Russia and Turkey have been historical enemies, fighting multiple wars over centuries. Iran and Turkey represent different branches of Islam and have competing regional ambitions. Yet shared opposition to Western influence and common hostility toward Israel have created unprecedented cooperation.

The military implications are staggering. Russian, Iranian, and Turkish forces have coordinated operations in Syria, directly on Israel's northern border. Joint military exercises have become routine. Intelligence sharing between these nations has reached levels that would have been unimaginable even a decade ago.

Russian President Putin has described his relationship with Iranian President Pezeshkian as reflecting "a very close worldview." A comprehensive Russia-Iran treaty that includes defense components was finalized in 2024. Turkey, despite its NATO membership, has increasingly aligned its foreign policy with Moscow and Tehran rather than Washington and Brussels.

Biblical scholars note the statement in Ezekiel 38:15 that the invasion will come specifically "from the north parts," which is exactly where these allied forces now position themselves relative to Israel. The prophet could not have provided a more precise geographic or political description of today's emerging coalition.

These developments are not chance or haphazard. Events in the Middle East continue to unfold just as we should expect if we consult the biblical end-time template. The buildup continues.

We can't be sure how long the buildup will last. Recent years have seen dramatic acceleration, with events moving at unprecedented speed. Yet the ultimate fulfillment of Ezekiel's prophecy, the great invasion of Israel by the Russian-Islamic coalition, still awaits God's appointed time. What we do know is that events in our world, especially in the Middle East, foreshadow and set the stage for the prophecies laid out in the pages of the Bible.

As we observe these developments in 2026 and beyond, the pieces of Ezekiel's prophetic puzzle continue falling into place with stunning precision. Iran's nuclear threshold status creates the existential pressure that could drive it toward the desperate alliance Ezekiel predicted. The Abraham Accords provide Israel with the security partnerships that allow it to enjoy some degree of security despite regional threats. The October 7 attacks and subsequent conflicts have weakened Iran's proxy network, making nuclear weapons seem more necessary for Iranian survival. Syria's transformation has disrupted old alliances while strengthening new ones that align exactly with biblical prophecy.

Most remarkably, the Russia-Iran-Turkey coalition now exists as a military reality for the first time in human history. These forces coordinate operations on Israel's northern border, precisely matching Ezekiel's geographic description. The convergence of nuclear weapons technology, regional realignments, and ancient alliances creates conditions that previous generations could never have imagined.

Yet we must remember that these are still the movements behind the curtain, the preparation for God's drama of the ages. The ultimate fulfillment of Ezekiel 38 awaits God's appointed time. Until then, we watch with the eyes of faith, understanding that current events are not accidental but providential—part of a divine plan revealed long ago. The stage is being set, the players are taking their positions.

Through God's Word we can see beyond the headlights. But what can we see?

FROM HEADLIGHTS TO THE SPOTLIGHT

Scripture shines a prophetic spotlight squarely on the Middle East, especially on the nation of Israel, but also on those who oppose Israel at the end of days. The scriptural spotlight reveals a cast of characters and places embedded in a storyline that is part of the script that moves the biblical story to its predicted climax.

Prominent in this story is Iran, which is arguably the world's most dangerous, provocative nation. Though Iran has faced significant military setbacks, it remains deeply committed to its objectives and continues to pose an existential threat to Israel and regional stability.[14]

Authors Charles Dyer and Mark Tobey have observed:

> Since the founding of the Islamic Republic, Iran has displayed a consistent commitment to two major goals. The first is to support the expansion of militant Islam, especially Shiite Islam. . . . Iran's second goal is the destruction of Israel, which they refer to as the "Zionist entity" and the "Little Satan". . . . The world might not take its threats seriously, but Iran has made no secret of its ambitions. Iran's leaders want to re-create the Persian Empire of old, but with an Islamic twist. They desire an arc of Shiite control stretching from Iran to the Mediterranean. They hope to become the dominant Muslim power in the Middle East . . . But to reach that goal they need to find a way to eliminate Israel.

> And that is where Iran's desires may intersect Bible prophecy.[15]

Succinctly stated, that's what this book is about: *the intersection of current events in Iran and the Middle East with Bible prophecy.* The following chapters will demonstrate that the converging and aligning of current events corresponds with the prophetic preview presented in Scripture.

As we observe and evaluate current events and world headlines, there are three key factors to keep in mind. First, the world is ever changing. Change is the new constant. There will be many twists and turns in the days ahead. We must be careful not to speculate about every interesting headline and its possible role in the end times. Recent history has demonstrated this truth vividly. Wars have erupted and paused. Leaders have fallen. Alliances have shifted. Yet through all the changes, the underlying prophetic trajectory remains clear and consistent.

Second, we must always evaluate current events in light of the Bible, and not the other way around. The Bible is our fixed point. To accurately discern if and how any current events fit into the prophetic picture, we need to understand Bible prophecy.

Third, events we see today are not the final fulfillment of Bible prophecy. The curtain has not been raised on God's drama of the ages. God is still setting the stage behind the curtain, providentially moving the props and players into place. When everything is finally in place and the time is right, the curtain will go up.

The raising of the curtain will take place, suddenly and without warning, at an event called the *rapture*, which is described in 1 Thessalonians 4:16–17 and is the next event on God's prophetic calendar. At the rapture, Jesus Christ, the Son of God, will come for His church, those who have believed in Him for salvation. In the time it takes to blink, He will meet His people in the air and whisk them away to heaven. The rapture is an imminent, unannounced event. No prophecy remains to be fulfilled before we could see the rapture. It could happen at any time—possible any day, impossible no day.

The curtain can go up at any moment.

THE EDGE OF TOMORROW

When it happens, the rapture will shock the world, because unexpectedly, millions of people will simply be missing. Spouses and children, rich and poor, soldiers and pastors, beggars and businesspeople—gone without a trace. As you can imagine, in the aftermath, people will search for some semblance of stability and security. The world will be gripped with fear. Confusion will reign. Then a strong-man, known in Scripture as the Antichrist, will arise amid the chaos from a Western confederacy, with answers and solutions. He'll be the man with a plan. He will ascend on a platform of peace and will forge a seven-year peace pact for Israel and her neighbors, one that will bring a palpable harmony to the Middle East. The Antichrist will be hailed by the world. He may even win the Nobel Peace Prize. Under his treaty, for the first time in her modern history, Israel will let down her guard and depend on the West for security. People everywhere will enjoy peace and safety . . . yet it will be but the calm before the storm.

From that point on, a series of catastrophic events will engulf the world. The Persian Storm, accompanied by many allies, will attempt to deliver a final, crushing blow to Israel, only to be supernaturally destroyed. This will pave the way for the balance of power to swing decisively in favor of the Western leader—the Antichrist. He will break his seven-year treaty with Israel at its midpoint and quickly begin consolidating power. During the final three and a half years of what is known as the Tribulation period, he will rule the world politically, militarily, and religiously. He will even go as far as to deify himself and demand worship. In the meantime, a series of devastating geological and ecological disasters will pummel the planet. The end of days will climax at the final great Battle of Armageddon when Jesus returns to defeat the Antichrist and his forces and establish His righteous kingdom on earth for one thousand years.

As astounding as the prophecies are, world events are moving toward their fulfillment. Nations are moving into place. World events are setting the stage. The escalating crisis in the Middle East fueled by Iran is an integral part of the buildup.

SEARCHING FOR ANSWERS

Everywhere we turn, ancient prophecies seem pregnant, ready to deliver and give birth to the end of the age, raising a chorus of compelling questions.

- Are current events in Iran and the Middle East part of a larger drama scripted long ago?
- Does the Bible predict the rise of Iran in the end times?
- What about Syria, Turkey, and Russia in the end of days?
- Where is the continuing crisis headed?
- Will Israel survive?
- What role will America play in the end of days?
- How should we live in light of current events?

As Christians, are we discerning enough to know what's coming? Will we be ready? Will you be ready? Bible prophecy was not given to scare us but to prepare us. It was not given to make us anxious but to make us alert and aware.

Two days before He died, Jesus told His closest followers, "Be on guard! Be alert! You do not know when that time will come." Then, comparing Himself to a master on a journey, He added, "Therefore keep watch because you do not know when the owner of the house will come back—whether in the evening, or at midnight, or when the rooster crows, or at dawn. If he comes suddenly, do not let him find you sleeping. What I say to you, I say to everyone: 'Watch!'" (Mark 13:33, 35–37 NIV).

Jesus wants us all to live looking.

The following pages are intended to increase your watchfulness and awareness of what lies ahead and to prepare you for the coming of Jesus. It is my hope that they will help you live faithfully in the meantime as you look for the endtime—as you endeavor to see beyond the headlights.

Whether you're reading this book for the first time or returning to it after world events have continued to unfold, the message remains the same: Bible prophecy is reliable, God is sovereign, and Jesus is coming soon.

So, grab your Bible, and let's get started.

CHAPTER 1

COUNTDOWN TO CRISIS

The Zionist regime will be uprooted from the region. This is certain.

—*Ayatollah Ali Khamenei,*
Iran's Supreme Leader, November 2024

If not stopped, Iran could produce a nuclear weapon in a very short time.

—*Israeli Prime Minister Benjamin Netanyahu,*
June 13, 2025

Iran could resume uranium enrichment in a matter of months.

—*Rafael Grossi,* IAEA Director General, June 2025

THE SHOWDOWN BETWEEN THE UNITED STATES, Israel, and Iran has moved from shadow war to shooting war and back again multiple times over the past several years. The question is no longer *if* major conflict will erupt, but when the next round will begin—and whether it will be the final one.

The tension has been building for decades, but the pace has accelerated dramatically. What was once measured in carefully calculated moves on a geopolitical chessboard has become a rapid succession of strikes, counterstrikes, and near-misses that threaten to spiral out of control at any moment.

In January 2020, a US drone strike killed Iranian Major General Qasem Soleimani, commander of Iran's elite Islamic Revolutionary Guard Corps Quds Force, as he arrived at Baghdad International Airport.[1] Soleimani was arguably the most powerful military leader in the Middle East; with the exception of Supreme Leader Ayatollah Ali Khamenei, he was the most important person in Iran. Iran immediately threatened revenge, and the world held its breath. War seemed imminent. Iran fired missiles at Iraqi bases housing American troops, causing over a hundred traumatic brain injuries among US service members, though no immediate fatalities.[2] The crisis appeared to de-escalate.

But the threat of Iranian retaliation never disappeared. In the years following Soleimani's death, US intelligence uncovered multiple Iranian plots to assassinate American officials, including President Trump himself, as well as former Secretary of State Mike Pompeo and National Security Adviser John Bolton.[3] The shadow war continued.

Then came October 7, 2023, when the regional dynamics shifted dramatically. As you'll recall, that's when Hamas, a key Iranian proxy, launched a coordinated surprise attack on Israel, killing more than 1,200 people, taking 251 hostages, and reshaping the entire Middle East landscape.[4]

As Israel prosecuted its war against Hamas in Gaza, it also turned its attention to Iran's other proxies. By early 2025, Hezbollah's military capabilities had been significantly degraded, with much of its leadership structure decimated and its arsenal of missiles substantially reduced.

The showdown that had been cooking for decades finally boiled over into direct confrontation, when Iran launched its first-ever direct missile attack on Israeli territory in April 2024, firing over three hundred projectiles including ballistic missiles and drones.[5] Israel, with assistance from the United States and regional partners, intercepted most of the incoming fire. Israel retaliated days later with strikes on Iranian targets. The conflict continued to escalate throughout 2024 and into 2025.

Then came Operation Rising Lion. In June 2025, the world's attention was locked again onto this region as Israel launched its massive surprise attack on Iran itself, striking nuclear facilities, military bases, and key infrastructure and assassinating top Iranian military commanders.[6] There was further awe and amazement when the United States joined the conflict days later, bombing Iran's most fortified nuclear sites with massive bunker busters.[7]

When the ceasefire was negotiated after twelve days of heavy fighting and hundreds of airstrikes,[8] and the guns fell silent, everyone realized this was not the end. It was merely a pause. The fundamental issues remained unresolved, and still do. Iran continues to enrich uranium. Israel continues to strike Iranian targets. The United States continues to impose sanctions. And the prophecies of Ezekiel continue to cast their shadow over the entire region.

THE RACE AGAINST TIME

Underlying all this military maneuvering is the one terrifying reality I mentioned earlier: Iran's nuclear program has reached critical mass.

You'll recall that by mid-2025, Iran had stockpiled over 400 kilograms of uranium enriched to 60 percent purity, which is just below the 90 percent threshold needed for nuclear weapons.[9] According to the IAEA, this is enough fissile material for more than a dozen nuclear weapons if further enriched.[10]

Even more alarming were the intelligence assessments indicating that Iran's "breakout time"—the period needed to enrich enough uranium for one nuclear weapon—has shrunk from twelve months to less than one week,[11] which was considered "effectively zero" by some analysts. By June 2025, when the IAEA formally found Iran to be in breach of its nuclear safeguards obligations for the first time since 2005,[12] the international community had run out of diplomatic options. This is what prompted Israel's decision to strike. Israeli leaders concluded they were almost out of time to prevent an Iranian bomb.

The June 2025 attacks set Iran's nuclear program back by months, perhaps a year or two, but did not eliminate it.[13] Rafael Grossi, director general of the IAEA, stated that Iran could resume uranium enrichment "in a matter of months."[14]

The clock is still ticking. Israel knows it cannot allow a regime that daily calls for its destruction to possess nuclear weapons. Iran knows that nuclear weapons are its only guarantee of survival against superior Israeli and American military power. Neither side can afford to back down. The collision course continues.

The ongoing crisis with Iran has created deep concern among Americans and allies about the potential for wider regional conflict. Again, the question on many minds is not *if* tensions will escalate once more, but when—and how devastating the next round will be.

PROPHETIC FLASH POINTS

The United States and Iran, however, are far from alone in the surging showdown. The Middle East neighborhood has become very crowded in the last few years, increasing the chances and raising the stakes for a major regional conflict as nations and terror groups stake out their turf and jockey for position.

The October 7, 2023, Hamas attack and subsequent Gaza war dramatically accelerated these tensions. Iran's proxy forces—Hamas in Gaza, Hezbollah in Lebanon, the Houthis in Yemen, and Shiite militias in Iraq—all mobilized in varying degrees.[15] Israel struck back hard, severely weakening much of Iran's carefully constructed "axis of resistance."

Saudi Arabia and Iran, close neighbors across the Persian Gulf, have long been bitter rivals. Their competition for regional dominance has erupted into numerous proxy conflicts across the Middle East—from Yemen and Syria to Lebanon and Iraq. The two nations came perilously close to direct war in September 2019, when Iranian-made drones and cruise missiles struck Saudi Arabia's Abqaiq and Khurais oil processing facilities. This temporarily knocked out half of the kingdom's crude production and caused the largest single disruption in global oil supply history.[16] The coordinated attack demonstrated Iran's capacity to strike with precision deep inside enemy territory, bypassing sophisticated air defenses and striking strategic infrastructure more than 700 kilometers from Iranian soil.[17] The US government and Saudi intelligence later presented forensic evidence linking the projectiles to Iran, concluding the assault was "an act of war."[18] This display of precision long-range capability would later be echoed in the June 2025 strikes against Israel, when Iranian missiles and drones once again showcased their range, coordination, and lethality.[19]

Underlying all of Iran's aggression is a dark, apocalyptic religious ideology deeply rooted in the worldview of the ruling clerical elite, the "mullahcracy" that governs the Islamic Republic. Since 1979, the regime has interpreted politics through a distinctly Shiite messianic lens, centered on belief in the eventual reappearance of the Twelfth Imam, also known as the Mahdi. According to Shia eschatology, the Mahdi will return amid global chaos and warfare to establish divine justice.[20] This conviction is not a fringe notion but one embedded in the theological writings and political rhetoric of Iran's highest leaders, including former President Mahmoud Ahmadinejad and former leader Ayatollah Ali Khamenei.[21] In this apocalyptic framework, conflict and crisis are not merely tolerated—they are instruments believed to hasten the Mahdi's advent.[22]

This ideology fuels Tehran's willingness to provoke confrontation with the United States and Israel, casting its geopolitical struggles in sacred, cosmic terms. Iranian hardliners openly frame military resistance as participation in a divinely mandated struggle against what they call the "arrogant powers" of the West and the "Zionist entity."[23] The regime's Revolutionary Guard (IRGC) and proxy militias translate this theology into action, pursuing a strategy of perpetual confrontation that keeps the Middle East on edge and pushes the region toward the brink of the very chaos their doctrine anticipates.[24] In this sense, Iran's apocalyptic vision is not abstract—it is the ideological engine behind its aggression, its sponsorship of proxy warfare, and its reckless ambition to ignite an end-times confrontation.

After thirteen long years of war, Syria's blood-soaked civil conflict reached its breaking point in December 2024.

Rebel forces swept into Damascus almost overnight, and Bashar al-Assad—the dictator whose family had ruled since 1970—fled to Russia. The fall of the Assad regime redrew the map of the Middle East and sent shockwaves through Iran's alliance network.[25] Assad fled to Russia, ending more than fifty years of his family's rule. This was a significant strategic defeat for Iran, severing its land corridor to Hezbollah and diminishing its influence in Syria. Iran, however, continues to seek ways to maintain its presence in the region. Meanwhile, Turkey has moved into Syria, right on Israel's northern border, filling the void left by the Russian and Iranian withdrawal as a result of their own struggles at home.

As you can see, potential, prophetic flashpoints abound. The drumbeat of war reverberates through the Middle East. One wrong move could set off a firestorm. All signs point to an imminent conflict. A buildup is brewing. At the center of the showdown stands Iran. Tehran's fingerprints can be found in the Strait of Hormuz, Yemen, Iraq, Lebanon, Gaza, and Syria. Everyone knows war is coming to the Middle East. The standoff could stir up into a storm at any moment.

ISRAEL IN THE CROSSHAIRS

Meanwhile, Israel sits at the epicenter of the region, no longer merely watching but actively striking. The "ring of fire" that Iran constructed around Israel—Hamas in

Gaza, Hezbollah in Lebanon, militias in Syria and Iraq, Houthis in Yemen—has been humiliated.

Israel and Iran are engaged in what may be described as a multi-round boxing match. Round one was fought through proxies. Round two included limited direct strikes in April 2024. Round three, the June 2025 war, saw the gloves come off entirely, with massive Israeli and American strikes on Iranian territory met by Iranian missile barrages against Israel.[26]

Israel and Iran are locked in a ferocious struggle that risks spiraling beyond control. As Iran pushes forward with sophisticated missile development and edges closer to nuclear capability, Israeli defense planners warn of increasing pressure on their home front. An EU think tank observed after the June 2025 conflict that Israel, Iran, and the United States appear to be bracing for further escalation, especially along Israel's borders, as the strategic environment has shifted dramatically.[27]

In Israel, the normal attitude of preparedness is quickly shifting to alarm. Israel knows it must be ready to strike Iran at any time. Israel can't let a nation that daily calls for its destruction get its hands on a nuclear missile. The winds of war are swirling. Storm clouds are gathering. Rumors of wars abound. Israel and Iran are on a collision course. War is coming. Again, it's not a matter of *if* but *when*. According to the nonpartisan, internationally focused Institute for Defence Studies and Analyses, "The tenuous ceasefire following the June 2025 12-Day War between Israel and Iran seems to be fraying at the seams. Fears of a new round of hostilities, if not an all-out war, have increased since late August.," meaning August 2025.[28]

A steady stream of ominous world headlines underscores the snowballing showdown with Iran:

- "Israel Launches Airstrikes on Iran's Nuclear Program, Killing Top Military Officials"—*The Guardian*, June 13, 2025.
- "Iran Fires Hundreds of Missiles and Drones at Israel in Retaliation"—Reuters, June 14, 2025.
- "Israel Hits Tehran with Intense Strikes"—*AP News*, June 17, 2025.
- "Israel's Airstrikes Aim to Break Foundations of Khamenei's Rule in Iran"—Reuters, June 19, 2025.
- "Israel-Iran War Enters Second Week with More Strikes"—CBS News, June 21, 2025.
- "Israel Prepared for a Long Campaign Against Iran"—*Al Jazeera*, June 21, 2025.
- "Visualizing Twelve Days of the Israel-Iran Conflict"—*Al Jazeera*, June 26, 2025.
- "Iran's Allies Across the Region Mobilize as Middle East Tensions Boil"—*New York Times*, July 2, 2025.
- "Aftershocks from the Israel-Iran War Reshape the Middle East"—*Foreign Policy*, July 15, 2025.
- "War Between Israel and Iran May Only Be in Pause, Not Over"—*Wall Street Journal*, August 10, 2025.
- "Another Israel-Iran War Increasingly Seen as

Just a Matter of Time"—*The Times of Israel*, November 10, 2025

- "Many Israelis Believe Another War with Iran Is Coming"—*The Economist*, November 27, 2025.

As tensions rise, world leaders continue to issue hollow calls for restraint, diplomacy, and de-escalation—yet everyone senses how quickly that could change. The region sits on a knife's edge. "One miscalculation could ignite a regional inferno that drags the entire Middle East into war," warns former Israeli national security adviser Yaakov Amidror.[29]

The clock is ticking. The countdown has begun—not just toward another Middle East war, but toward something greater. The storm gathering over Israel and Iran feels eerily familiar to those who understand Bible prophecy. Could these tremors be the first rumblings of the final conflict foretold in Scripture? Could the countdown to conflict also be the countdown to the fulfillment of ancient prophecies?

WHAT'S NEXT?

The June 2025 war answered some questions but raised many more. Iran's nuclear program was set back but not destroyed. Its military leadership was decimated but will be replaced. And Iran's proxy network, though weakened, remains dangerous.

More importantly, Iran's fundamental ideology has

not changed. The regime still calls for Israel's destruction. It still pursues regional hegemony. It still seeks nuclear weapons as the ultimate guarantee of survival and tool of intimidation.

Israel, for its part, has demonstrated both its capability and its willingness to strike deep inside Iran. The taboo against direct military confrontation has been shattered. What was once unthinkable has become routine.

Several scenarios could trigger the next major escalation:

- **IRAN'S NUCLEAR RESTART:** Despite severe damage, Iran retains the knowledge, personnel, and some infrastructure to rebuild its nuclear program. If Tehran decides to sprint toward a nuclear weapon, Israel has made clear it will strike again—and harder.
- **PROXY REACTIVATION:** Though degraded, Iran's proxy forces throughout the region remain intact. Hamas has been weakened but not entirely eliminated. Hezbollah has been set back but still possesses substantial military capabilities. The Houthis in Yemen continue to launch attacks. Any of these groups could spark a wider conflict.
- **IRANIAN RETALIATION:** Iran has a long history of seeking revenge, even years after initial provocations. Following the Soleimani killing in 2020, Iran pursued numerous plots to assassinate American

officials. Similar efforts to avenge the losses of June 2025 are likely already underway.[30]

- **ECONOMIC DESPERATION:** Iran's economy continues to suffer under international sanctions. Domestic unrest threatens the regime's stability. Desperate leaders sometimes make desperate choices, including military adventurism to unite the nation against external enemies.
- **SYRIAN INSTABILITY:** With Assad gone, Syria's future remains uncertain. Various factions, including Turkish-backed forces, Kurdish groups, and remnants of Iranian influence, compete for control. This instability could provide opportunities for Iran to regain a foothold—or spark conflicts that draw in multiple regional powers.

The prophets of the Bible tell us that a great war is coming to the Middle East, a war involving Russia, Iran, Turkey, and other nations in a massive invasion of Israel described in Ezekiel 38–39. Recent events have demonstrated that such a scenario is not only possible but increasingly plausible. The nations are aligning. The animosities are intensifying. The stage is being set.

We're witnessing the buildup. The final thunderstorm still lies ahead.

CHAPTER 2

ATOMIC IRAN AND THE APOCALYPSE

> Iran may still have 400 kilograms of highly enriched uranium. How worried should we be?
>
> —*The Times of Israel (July 2025)*

APPEARING ON NBC'S *Meet the Press* in 2006, when asked what would happen if Iran gets the nuclear bomb, Senator John McCain responded, "I think we could have Armageddon."[1] Undoubtedly, he expressed the fear of many people if Iran were to go nuclear. Those fears expressed twenty years ago, while somewhat allayed in recent months, are still real. Few events would change the world as dramatically as Iran getting its hands on a deliverable nuclear weapon. Israel would immediately face an existential threat. Iran's leaders have regularly spewed out statements like this one from supreme leader Ayatollah Khamenei: "The belief that Israel must be eliminated is a condition of our adherence to Islam. . . . Each and every one of our officials should reiterate our responsibility of the need to destroy this cancerous tumor of Israel."[2] This leaves little doubt of what Iran would do if it obtained the bomb, and recent events may have propelled Iran closer to the nuclear threshold than ever before. Backed into a corner, Iran may believe that a nuclear breakout is their last line of defense.

So let's review—with a little more detail—the timeline we've been observing in the trajectory of Iran's nuclear program.

That trajectory accelerated dramatically after the United States withdrew from the Joint Comprehensive Plan of Action (JCPOA) in 2018 and reimposed sanctions. Iran responded by progressively abandoning the deal's restrictions, ramping up uranium enrichment and expanding its centrifuge operations.

The assassination of Iranian Major General Qasem Soleimani in January 2020 marked another turning point, prompting Iran to announce it would no longer observe any limitations on enrichment. In the wake of his death, Iranian President Hassan Rouhani's administration declared, "The country will not observe limitations on its enrichment, the amount of stockpiled enriched uranium, as well as research and development in its nuclear activities."[3] From that moment, Iran's nuclear program advanced with alarming speed.

As we've seen, Iran by 2023 was crossing critical thresholds that once seemed distant. The nation began enriching uranium to 60 percent purity, just a technical step away from the 90 percent needed for weapons-grade material. Intelligence agencies that once measured Iran's "breakout time" in years, then months, now speak of weeks or even days.[4] The breakout timeline that was "seven to eleven months" in 2020 had shrunk to effectively zero by 2025.

The situation reached a crisis point in mid-2025 when Iran's stockpile of 60 percent enriched uranium exceeded 400 kilograms, which is enough material for more than a dozen nuclear weapons if further enriched.[5] This, combined with Iran's continued refusal to cooperate with IAEA inspectors, left the international community with diminishing options.

In addition to the existential threat this poses for Israel, if Iran obtains nukes, most experts believe it will throw the door wide open for an all-out nuclear arms race in the Middle East. It would set off a chain reaction with Turkey and Saudi Arabia following close behind. Iran is the fuse on an explosive nuclear powder keg. In January 2024, the Bulletin of the Atomic Scientists set the Doomsday Clock at ninety seconds to midnight, the closest it has ever been to symbolic catastrophe.[6] Then just one year later in 2025 it was moved one second closer—eighty-nine seconds to midnight. The June 2025 Israeli-Iranian confrontation vindicated their warning. The world came closer to nuclear conflict in the Middle East than at any time since these weapons were first developed.

Another dangerous angle is that for some time North Korea has been a key supplier of missile technology to Iran. This raises the fear that Iran could procure a ready-made nuclear weapon from North Korea, or that the two rogue nations could collaborate on weapons development.[7]

As Israeli Major General Yaakov Amidror warned years ago, "With a nuclear umbrella, Iran would be free to build a ring of fire around Israel," at which point it would be too late for Jerusalem to stop either the nuclear program or Iran's destabilizing behavior in the region.[8]

That prediction proved prophetic. Time ran out, and Israel acted. In June 2025, faced with Iran's approach to nuclear weapons capability, Israel launched Operation Rising Lion with massive strikes against Iranian nuclear facilities. The United States joined days later with attacks on Iran's most fortified sites with devastating "bunker buster" bombs.[9] The strikes set Iran's program back significantly, but IAEA Director General Rafael Grossi warned that Iran could resume uranium enrichment "in a matter of months."[10]

The question is no longer theoretical. Now it's operational: Can Israel and the international community prevent Iran from obtaining nuclear weapons, or has the world entered a new era where a nuclear-armed Iran becomes inevitable? And if Iran does obtain the bomb, what will that mean for Israel's survival and the fulfillment of Bible prophecy in the Middle East?

DECADES IN THE MAKING

Iran's love affair with the bomb goes back decades, at least to the 1980s. The United States and European nations have continuously pursued discussions, negotiations, and concessions with Tehran but with few lasting results. Iran clandestinely works on its nuclear program and employs a strategy of "talk and build." Using this tactic, Iran delays and strings along negotiations as it continues to advance toward the nuclear finish line.

Here's a chart of Iran's nuclear trajectory that adds a number of earlier developments:

IRAN'S NUCLEAR TIMELINE

1987	Iran acquired nuclear centrifuge technology from Dr. Abdul Qadeer Khan, a renegade Pakistani engineer.
January 1995	Russia signs an $800 million nuclear plant deal with Iran to complete the nuclear plant at Bushehr.
November 2004	Iran agrees to suspend uranium enrichment.
January 9, 2006	Rebuffed by European diplomatic efforts, Iran resumes uranium production at its plant in Natanz, claiming that its only intention is to make reactor fuel to generate electricity.
March 29, 2006	The UN Security Council unanimously approves a statement demanding that Iran suspend uranium enrichment.
April 9, 2006	Iran officially announces it has begun enriching uranium.

2009–2012	Rounds of sanctions and talks are conducted.
2012	Talk of an Israeli strike against Iran escalates amid renewed negotiations and strengthened sanctions.
2015	The heralded JCPOA, also known as the Iran nuclear deal, is signed by Iran and the P5+1 (United States, United Kingdom, France, China, Russia, and Germany).
2019	The United States backs out of the JCPOA and reinstates crippling economic sanctions on Iran. In response, Iran escalates its nuclear production.
2020	Iran pulls back its commitments to the nuclear deal in the wake of the US drone strike against Major General Qasem Soleimani, further reducing the time for a nuclear breakout to less than a year.
January 2020	US drone strike kills Iranian Major General Qasem Soleimani. Iran announces it will no longer observe any JCPOA limitations on enrichment.
2020–2023	Iran progressively expands uranium enrichment activities and centrifuge capacity while reducing IAEA access to facilities.
2023	Iran begins enriching uranium to 60 percent purity, approaching weapons-grade levels. Its stockpile grows rapidly.

October 7, 2023	Hamas launches surprise attack on Israel with Iranian backing, triggering regional war.
April 2024	Iran launches first-ever direct military attack on Israel with over 300 missiles and drones. Israel retaliates with strikes on Iranian targets.
September 2024	Israel assassinates Hezbollah leader Hassan Nasrallah, severely degrading Iran's primary proxy force.
December 2024	Syrian President Bashar al-Assad's regime collapses, severing Iran's land corridor to Lebanon and weakening its regional position.
May 2025	IAEA reports Iran's stockpile of 60 percent enriched uranium exceeds 400 kilograms—sufficient for more than a dozen weapons if further enriched.
June 2025	IAEA Board formally finds Iran in breach of nuclear safeguards obligations for first time since 2005.
June 13, 2025	Israel launches Operation Rising Lion—massive strikes against Iranian nuclear facilities, research centers, and military infrastructure.
June 22, 2025	United States conducts follow-up strikes on Iran's most fortified nuclear sites.

June 24, 2025	Ceasefire negotiated after twelve days of intense conflict. IAEA warns Iran could resume enrichment "in a matter of months."
October 13, 2025	Hamas releases all twenty remaining living Israeli hostages in exchange for 250 Palestinian prisoners and 1,700+ detainees. Trump travels to Israel and addresses the Knesset. Trump co-chairs international peace summit in Sharm el-Sheikh, Egypt, with President el-Sisi. Over twenty world leaders sign "The Trump Declaration for Enduring Peace and Prosperity." Iran invited but declines to attend. Trump signals willingness to lift sanctions on Iran if Tehran is willing to negotiate, stating, "I'd love to take the sanctions off when they're ready to talk."

TOXIC TALK

As Iran has worked feverishly to procure a nuclear weapon, its leaders continued their decades-long rhetoric about wiping Israel off the map. That's a potentially lethal combination. The inflammatory statements have continued even after Israel's devastating strikes against Iran's nuclear program and proxy network in 2024–2025. Here's a sample of what Iran's leaders have said about Israel over the years. If you're Israel, these are not people you can allow to get the bomb:

- **AYATOLLAH ALI KHAMENEI**: "It is the mission of the Islamic Republic of Iran to erase Israel from the map of the region." And: "The Zionist regime is a cancerous tumor and it will be removed." And in November 2024: "The Zionist regime will be uprooted from the region. This is certain."[11] And in June 2025, after Israeli strikes on Iranian nuclear facilities: "The criminal Zionist regime made a mistake in attacking Iran. They will certainly receive a response."[12]
- **HASSAN NASRALLAH**, leader of Hezbollah (killed by Israeli strike, September 27, 2024): "If they [Jews] all gather in Israel, it will save us the trouble of going after them worldwide." And: "Israel is our enemy. This is an aggressive, illegal, and illegitimate entity, which has no future in our land. Its destiny is manifested in our motto: 'Death to Israel.' "
- **MOHAMMAD HASSAN RAHIMIAN**, Khamenei's representative to the Moustazafan Foundation: "We have manufactured missiles that allow us, when necessary, to replace Israel in its entirety with a big holocaust."
- **MOHAMMAD REZA NAQDI**, commander of the Basij paramilitary force: "We recommend them [the Zionists] to pack their furniture and return to their countries. And if they insist on staying, they should know that a time will arrive when they will not even have time to pack their suitcases."

- **HOSSEIN SALAMI**, the deputy head of the Revolutionary Guard: "We will chase you [Israelis] house to house and will take revenge for every drop of blood of our martyrs in Palestine, and this is the beginning point of Islamic nations awakening for your defeat."[13]
- **HOSSEIN SHEIKHOLESLAM**, a foreign affairs adviser to parliamentary speaker Ali Larijani: "Our positions against the usurper Zionist regime have not changed at all; Israel should be annihilated and this is our ultimate slogan."[14]
- **IRANIAN PRESIDENT EBRAHIM RAISI** (October 2023, following Hamas attack): "The al-Aqsa Storm operation will be a turning point in the Palestinian struggle, and the Zionist regime has received an irreparable blow."[15]

These are just a few of the thousands of poisonous statements that have spewed forth from Iran and its proxies over the decades. You can almost feel the venom dripping from the page as they beat the drum for a second holocaust. Even after Israel decimated Hezbollah's leadership, degraded Hamas, and struck Iranian nuclear facilities in 2024–2025, the rhetoric continues unabated from Tehran. Iranian leaders remain committed to their stated goal of Israel's destruction—a commitment that makes the prospect of an Iranian nuclear weapon an existential threat not just to Israel, but to regional and global stability.

2025: CROSSING THE NUCLEAR THRESHOLD

The events of 2025 represent a critical inflection point in the four-decade showdown between Israel, the United States, and Iran. What was once theoretical—Iran possessing near-weapons-grade nuclear material—became reality.

Once more, let's review closely the factors we've seen that converged to make 2025 a decisive year:

1. Iran's uranium enrichment reached unprecedented levels. By mid–2025, Iran possessed over 400 kilograms of uranium enriched to 60 percent purity—a level that has no peaceful civilian purpose and sits just below the 90 percent threshold required for nuclear weapons.[16] The technical leap from 60 to 90 percent enrichment is relatively small, and experts concluded Iran could make this jump in days if it chose to do so.[17]
2. The IAEA issued its most serious rebuke of Iran in two decades. In June 2025, the IAEA Board of Governors formally found Iran in breach of its nuclear safeguards obligations for the first time since 2005.[18] This declaration signaled that diplomatic efforts had effectively failed, and Iran was operating its nuclear program with minimal international oversight.
3. Iran continued developing advanced centrifuges and expanding its nuclear infrastructure at

multiple sites, including the deeply buried Fordow facility. These developments significantly reduced Iran's "breakout time" (the period needed to produce enough fissile material for one nuclear weapon) to effectively zero.[19]

4. Regional dynamics shifted dramatically. The October 7, 2023, Hamas attack on Israel and the subsequent war in Gaza demonstrated Iran's willingness to use its proxy network for large-scale attacks. The September 2024 assassination of Hezbollah leader Hassan Nasrallah by Israel severely degraded but did not eliminate Iran's primary proxy force. These events convinced Israeli leaders that time was running out to prevent an Iranian bomb.[20]
5. The collapse of the Assad regime in Syria in December 2024 dealt a strategic blow to Iran, severing its land corridor to Hezbollah. Yet this setback also made Iranian leaders more desperate to secure their nuclear deterrent as their regional position weakened.[21]

Faced with these converging factors, Israel made the fateful decision to strike. On June 13, 2025, Israeli aircraft, supported by American intelligence and likely tactical assistance, conducted Operation Rising Lion with precision strikes against key Iranian nuclear facilities.[22] The attacks targeted enrichment sites, research facilities, and production infrastructure in an effort to set Iran's nuclear program back by months or years.

While the strikes inflicted considerable damage, they did not eliminate Iran's nuclear program. IAEA Director General Rafael Grossi warned that Iran could resume uranium enrichment "in a matter of months."[23] The fundamental problem remained: Iran possesses the knowledge, infrastructure, and materials to build nuclear weapons. The strikes bought time, but they did not resolve the crisis.

The aftermath of the June 2025 strikes brought a temporary ceasefire brokered by international mediators, but the underlying conflict remains unresolved.[24] Iran continues to pursue its nuclear ambitions, Israel maintains it cannot allow a nuclear-armed Iran, and both sides understand that the next round of confrontation could be the final one.

The question is no longer *whether* Iran will cross the nuclear threshold, but *when*—and what will happen when it does.

HOT-WIRING THE APOCALYPSE

The danger of Iran obtaining a nuclear weapon has always been exacerbated by the apocalyptic religious ideology that holds its leaders in its grip. The Iranian ayatollah and sinister mullahs hold to an alarming, eerie "Apocalypse Now" viewpoint. They're waiting for the return of their Mahdi or messiah, known as the "Twelfth Iman."

They believe they can accelerate the end of days and their final victory by creating chaos and bloodshed. Part of hastening the apocalypse is getting rid of the "Great Satan" (America) and the "Little Satan" (Israel). This adds a much deeper dimension to Iran's vitriol toward the United States and Israel, and Iran's nuclear pursuits. The clash is not just about power and geography, it's about Iran's realizing its messianic destiny.

Writing in the *Jerusalem Post*, Lela Gilbert unmasks the apocalyptic madness that undergirds Iran's pursuit of the bomb and overall aggressive posture.

> Why does Iran continue to saber-rattle and threaten to massacre Israelis? Why do Iranian religious and military leaders constantly vow to impose terrible violence on their enemies? And why is the ever-escalating aggression carried on by various Iranian proxies across the Middle East? These days, international commentators assume that threats of violence and warnings of war are Iran's boastful way of defying US economic sanctions, which now have a stranglehold on their leaders and institutions. Meanwhile, disturbances in the Persian Gulf have underscored the Islamic Republic's rage at America's withdrawal from the JCPOA. But there is, perhaps, another reason as well—an apocalyptic belief that is widely held by Iran's supreme leader and his followers.

Gilbert further states:

> The Hidden—or Twelfth—Imam plays a dominant role in one specific form of Shi'ite Islamic theology, called

> "Twelverism," which happens to be the primary belief system of Iran's leadership. There is a messianic belief that at the end of days, the Hidden Imam will appear in the midst of a violent apocalyptic scenario played out on a battleground stained with infidels' blood. . . .
>
> [Iranian scholar Saeed Ghasseminejad wrote,] "While many experts tell us Iran is a rational, pragmatic regime like any other in the world, all the facts shout that it is not. A large number of Iranian officials and decision makers have deeply rooted apocalyptic beliefs. Underestimating this radical ideology even as the Iranian regime is on its way to building a nuclear bomb can lead to dangerously wrong conclusions. The suggestion taking hold of late that a nuclear-armed Iran is not the end of the world may unfortunately be dead wrong."[25]

Israeli poet and writer Salman Masalha puts it poignantly: "The Islamic revolution, which brought the ayatollahs to power in Iran, awakened messianic demons from their sleep."[26] These awakened demons are on full display in Iran today. Those who understand the nexus between Iran's nuclear pursuits and its messianic demons have an additional incentive to keep Iran from getting weapons of mass destruction.

THE SYRIAN CONNECTION

Iran's former presence in Syria played significantly into its apocalyptic views and desire for nuclear weapons. For years, Iran maintained a substantial military presence in Syria for multiple strategic reasons—nearness to Israel's northern border, support for Bashar al-Assad's regime in the civil war that raged from 2011, and the creation of a "Shia crescent" from Iran to the Mediterranean. However, an often-forgotten reason for Iran's investment in Syria was the messianism that grips Iran's menacing mullahocracy. According to Twelver Shi'ism practiced in Iran, Syria holds special significance for Iran's messianic hopes.

Syria is important to Iran for messianic reasons because, according to Shi'ite traditions, the Mahdi's reincarnation is associated with a bloody civil war that will take place in Syria and cause hundreds of thousands of deaths. The prophecy describes a conflict that begins on a small scale and then escalates, seeming to calm in one area before bursting out in another, and continuing until the Mahdi appears.[27]

According to this tradition, when the Shi'ite Mahdi appears he will bear God's explicit name in Hebrew. He will also hold the staff of Moses, wear Solomon's seal, and carry the Israelites' ark of the covenant, in which the Divine Presence (*shekinah*) dwells. With the ark and the Divine Presence he will conquer cities and countries and impose law and justice in the world.[28]

For years, Iran viewed its expanding presence in Syria as the realization of a long-awaited messianic hope. Iranian leaders believed events were unfolding in keeping with their view of the end of days. Then came December 2024. Syria's brutal civil war, which had raged since 2011, came to a dramatic and unexpected conclusion when rebel forces toppled the Assad regime.[29] Assad fled to Russia, ending more than fifty years of his family's rule. The rapid collapse stunned the region and represented a catastrophic strategic defeat for Iran.

The fall of Assad severed Iran's land corridor to Hezbollah in Lebanon, which was the vital supply route through which Iran had armed and supported its most powerful proxy. Iran lost the military bases it had constructed across Syria. Russian forces, already stretched thin by their war in Ukraine, could not prevent the regime's collapse. In a matter of days, Iran's decades-long investment in Syria and its carefully constructed "Shia crescent" crumbled.

Yet Iran's messianic ideology remains unchanged. Iranian leaders still believe in the apocalyptic prophecies that originally drew them to Syria. They continue to seek ways to maintain influence in the region and to rebuild what was lost. The theological convictions that drove Iran's Syria strategy—the belief in hastening the Mahdi's return through warfare and bloodshed—have not disappeared with Assad's fall.

If anything, the strategic setbacks of 2024–2025 may make Iran more desperate and more dangerous. Having lost Syria, having seen Hezbollah decimated, and having endured strikes on its nuclear facilities, Iran's leaders face a stark choice: accept a diminished regional role or double down on their pursuit of nuclear weapons as the ultimate guarantor of survival and regional dominance.

The collapse of Assad's regime demonstrates that even carefully laid plans can unravel quickly in the volatile Middle East. But it does not change the underlying dynamics driving Iran toward confrontation. The messianic fervor, the commitment to Israel's destruction, and the pursuit of nuclear capability all remain. Only the playing field has shifted.

CONVERGING CONNECTIONS

Iran continues taking aggressive action to bring about the realization of its apocalyptic future, even as major setbacks reshape the regional landscape. The mullah regime, the Ayatollah's leadership, nuclear weapons pursuits, a violent end-of-days scenario, and intense hatred for Israel and the United States remain essential ingredients in this apocalyptic vision. Despite losing its Syrian ally, seeing Hezbollah degraded, and enduring strikes on its nuclear facilities, Iran has not abandoned its ultimate goals. At some point these ingredients will mingle in a toxic cocktail that will set in motion a series of events that will propel the world toward the fulfillment of ancient biblical prophecy. The question is whether Iran's recent defeats will delay or accelerate that confrontation.

But before we turn to the ancient forecast of the Hebrew prophet Ezekiel, there's one more volatile ingredient to add to the mixture.

CHAPTER 3

DIRE STRAITS

We have the capability to close the Strait of Hormuz. The decision rests with high-ranking officials, and the IRGC navy will act in accordance with orders., IRGC Navy Commander, February 2025

—*Rear Admiral Alireza Tangsiri,* Iranian Revolutionary Guard Corps, Navy Commander, February 2025

The Iranian regime would be foolish to make that decision.

—*Karoline Leavitt,* White House Press Secretary, on Iran closing the Strait of Hormuz, June 2025

To the Department of Energy: DRILL, BABY, DRILL!!! And I mean NOW!!! EVERYONE, KEEP OIL PRICES DOWN. I'M WATCHING! YOU'RE PLAYING RIGHT INTO THE HANDS OF THE ENEMY. DON'T DO IT!"

—*President Donald Trump,* June 2025

ACCORDING TO THE DICTIONARY, *dire straits* means "a state of extreme distress . . . a bad or difficult situation or state of affairs."[1] That's an apt description of the world's direst "strait": the situation in Iran's backyard involving the Strait of Hormuz, or SOH. A dark shadow looms over the waters of the strait as massive tankers traverse its narrow channel under Iran's watchful eye. Iran regularly threatens to close the strait in retaliation against US actions. This could be called the "Iranian shutdown," since the Strait of Hormuz is frequently crawling with Iranian speedboats that stand ready to swarm hostile vessels, shutting off the spigot of oil from the Persian Gulf. The Strait of Hormuz is a perennial international hotspot. It's been the focal point of US-Iranian confrontations for more than thirty years.

What makes it such a frequent flashpoint that shows up in the news on a regular basis?

The Strait of Hormuz is the number one shipping channel in the world. The narrow strait, which connects the Persian Gulf and the Gulf of Oman, lies along the western coast of Iran. Ships traversing the strait must pass through Iranian waters. It's the only sea passage from the oil-rich Persian Gulf to the open ocean. And Iran believes it owns the strait.

The SOH is a vital gateway for global oil supply. It's the world's most important oil transit chokepoint, involving about twenty-one million barrels of oil per day. "Roughly 27 percent of the world's crude oil and petroleum products maritime trade goes through the Strait.

Additionally, 22 percent of global liquefied natural gas trade passes through the Strait."[2]

The SOH is ninety-six miles long and twenty-one miles wide at its narrowest point; however, the shipping lanes in each direction are just two miles wide. This narrow area of operation provides Iran a major tactical advantage, making it easy to saturate with mines and swarm with speedboats.

HISTORICAL TENSIONS AND RECENT ESCALATIONS

The Strait of Hormuz has long been a flashpoint for US-Iranian confrontation. The tension-filled summer of 2019 epitomized the ongoing hostility when six oil tankers came under attack—two damaged by explosions after leaving the strait, and four struck within United Arab Emirates territorial waters. Iran diverted a British-flagged oil tanker to one of its ports in an action the UK called illegal, and shot down a US drone over the strait. The United States downed an Iranian drone that came too close to the USS *Boxer*. This dangerous "Game of Drones" brought the United States and Iran perilously close to a shooting war.[3]

In response to these provocations, the United States deployed an additional fourteen thousand troops to the region, including an aircraft carrier, and promised to strike back hard against any similar Iranian actions.[4]

The 2019 incidents demonstrated a pattern that has continued into the present: Iran uses the narrow strait as leverage against Western economic sanctions and as a means to flex its muscles, showing it can disrupt global oil flow by choking off access to the Persian Gulf. The strait remains Iran's most potent non-nuclear weapon. Iran holds it as a geographic advantage that allows it to threaten the world's energy supply with relatively limited military assets.

In recent years, tensions over the strait have evolved beyond isolated incidents. The broader regional conflict that erupted in October 2023 with Hamas's attack on Israel, followed by direct Iranian missile strikes on Israel in April 2024 and Israeli strikes on Iranian territory in June 2025, demonstrated that the theater of confrontation has expanded beyond the Persian Gulf. Yet the Strait of Hormuz remains a critical pressure point.

Russia and China continue to conduct joint naval exercises with Iran in the Gulf of Oman just outside the strait, bolstering Iran's image as a regional power backed by great powers.

China, Iran, and Russia held a "Maritime Security Belt 2025" naval exercise in the Gulf of Oman near the Strait of Hormuz, aimed at signaling unity and Iran's image as cooperating with the greater powers.[5] These exercises serve as a reminder that any conflict over the strait could draw in other major powers, potentially triggering a wider confrontation.

THE TANKER WAR

Skirmishes in the Persian Gulf between the United States and Iran are nothing new.

What we see today evokes memories of the tanker war more than thirty years ago when the SOH was the scene of a tense standoff between the United States and Iran.[6] During the 1980s, 40 percent of the world's oil passed through the Strait of Hormuz, so any disruption, no matter how slight, threatened to create chaos in the global oil market.

The tanker war was waged from 1984 to 1988 during the Iran-Iraq War as Iran picked off Kuwaiti vessels transporting Iraq's oil to market. Kuwait persuaded US President Ronald Reagan to reflag and escort its vessels through the Strait of Hormuz. In the spring of 1988, an Iranian mine disabled and nearly sank the USS *Samuel B. Roberts*. In response to Iran's actions, open conflict between the United States and Iran erupted on April 18, 1988. The United States waged an intense one-day battle against Iranian forces in and around the strait. The US-Iran shooting match resulted in the disabling of several Iranian warships.

In some ways the tanker war between the United States and Iran never ended. It was just indefinitely suspended. Both sides stopped shooting, but nothing was really settled or resolved. It was simply a perilous prelude to what's happening in the Persian Gulf today and what will inevitably persist in the future.

FROM PRELUDE TO PROPHECY

The Strait of Hormuz has remained at the center of escalating tensions between the United States, Israel, and Iran for decades. From the tanker wars of the late 1980s through the confrontations of 2019 and beyond, the strait has been and continues to be a major danger zone. The difference now is that the regional dynamics have fundamentally shifted.

Iran is no longer merely threatening to close the strait or harassing tankers. In April 2024, Iran launched its first-ever direct military attack on Israeli territory, firing a barrage of over three hundred missiles and drones at Israel from Iranian soil.[7] While most were intercepted with help from the United States and regional partners, the attack shattered the long-standing pattern of Iran working exclusively through proxies. Iran had crossed a threshold, demonstrating its willingness to strike directly at Israel despite the risks.

Israel responded in kind, and the tit-for-tat escalation culminated in June 2025 with Operation Rising Lion—Israel's massive strikes against Iranian nuclear facilities and military infrastructure,[8] then American follow-up strikes on Iran's most fortified nuclear sites. Despite the ceasefire brokered after twelve days of hard fighting, nothing was truly resolved.[9]

In this new reality, the Strait of Hormuz takes on even greater significance. Iran's regional position has been severely weakened. It lost its Syrian ally when the Assad regime collapsed in December 2024. Its most powerful proxy, Hezbollah, was decimated by Israeli strikes that killed longtime leader Hassan Nasrallah and destroyed much of the organization's military infrastructure. Its nuclear program, while not eliminated, was set back significantly by the June 2025 strikes.

Remember that a weakened Iran may be even more dangerous than a confident one. With fewer strategic options, Iran could see the strait as its remaining leverage, the geographic chokepoint where it still holds tactical advantage. The narrow waters give Iran the ability to threaten global energy supplies with relatively modest military assets: mines, swarms of fast boats, anti-ship missiles, and drones. In a confrontation where Iran is losing ground on every other front, the strait becomes both a last resort and a tempting target.

Never missing an opportunity to threaten Israel, Iran continues to use tensions in the Strait of Hormuz as a platform for intimidation and escalation. In the wake of renewed maritime clashes in 2025, senior Iranian commanders have warned that if Israel or its allies interfere in the strait, Tel Aviv and Haifa will face destruction within minutes.[10] These threats came as Iran's navy, alongside Russian and Chinese vessels, conducted joint drills in the Gulf of Oman—an unmistakable display of force meant to signal that any conflict in the waters off Iran's southern coast could rapidly expand into a regional confrontation.[11]

Iran's naval chief, Admiral Shahram Irani, declared in January 2026 that the Islamic Republic's forces were on "full readiness" to respond to any Israeli presence in the strait.[12] These provocations serve as a stark reminder: The Strait of Hormuz remains one of the world's most dangerous flashpoints, where a single miscalculation could ignite a war drawing in multiple global powers.

As Iranian Foreign Minister Mohammad Javad Zarif warned years ago, "We always respond. Don't play with Iran."[13] That statement has proven prophetic. Iran's "eye-for-an-eye" strategy of payback has been on full display in recent years, from the April 2024 missile strikes to ongoing threats against American officials and continued support for attacks on Israel through its remaining proxies.

The Strait of Hormuz will continue to be a critical staging ground for potential conflict between the United States, its allies, and Iran. One reckless move by any party could reignite open warfare, but this time the stakes are immeasurably higher than they were in 1988 or even 2019. Iran is backed into a corner, has demonstrated its willingness to strike directly at adversaries, and retains control over the world's most vital energy chokepoint.

As the Middle East buildup to the end times gains momentum, as prophesied by Ezekiel and other biblical writers, the Strait of Hormuz will undoubtedly play a significant role. It is not just a shipping lane—it is a powder keg, and the fuse grows shorter with each passing confrontation.

CHAPTER 4

THE PERSIA PROPHECIES

The past is never dead. It's not even past.

—*William Faulkner, Requiem for a Nun*

IN HIS PLAY *The Tempest*, Shakespeare's character Antonio utters the now-famous words, "What's past is prologue." In contemporary use, the phrase means that history creates the context for the present. That what has happened in the past sets the stage for the present and future.

What's true in general is especially true in biblical prophecy. Historical events often set up the future and even repeat themselves. They recapitulate and replicate established patterns. Biblical prophecies dealing with Persia are no exception. Iran's past is prologue to what we see today, and also to what's coming in the future.

The ancient Persian Empire was impressive. It conquered Babylon, under the rule of King Cyrus and ruled over a huge swath of territory for about two hundred years (539–331 BC). The empire ruled over two million square miles, stretching from Egypt to India. As we're witnessing Iran's attempt to birth a new Persian Empire, it's important to briefly look back at biblical prophecies about Persia that have already been fulfilled to see what they can tell us, if anything, about what we see today and what we can expect tomorrow.

PRESENTING PERSIA

The word *Iran* never appears in the Bible in any end-time prophecies, but the name of its ancient counterpart, *Persia*, in its various forms, is found thirty-six times in the Old Testament. In recent times the name Persia was changed to Iran, which means "land of the Aryans," and then was later changed to the Islamic Republic of Iran.

Many occurrences of the word *Persia* in Scripture are simply historical references, but there are several fascinating biblical prophecies about Persia that have already come to fulfillment. The past fulfillment of prophecies about Persia is prologue to what we see today. Knowing the literal fulfillment of past prophecies establishes the trajectory for the fulfillment of future prophecies.

DANIEL: THE RISE AND FALL OF THE PERSIAN EMPIRE

The Jewish prophet Daniel lived in the sixth century B.C. during the Babylonian Empire and the early years of the

Persian Empire. The book of Daniel contains three main prophecies about ancient Persia that have been fulfilled in the ancient past.

DANIEL 2: SILVER SHOULDERS

Daniel 2 recounts a dream of Nebuchadnezzar, king of Babylon, given to him by God. The meaning of the dream was interpreted by Daniel the prophet. Nebuchadnezzar's dream involved a colossal statue of a man consisting of four different metals: gold (the head), silver (the shoulders and arms), bronze (the belly and thighs), and iron (the legs). The feet of the image consisted of a mixture of iron and clay. Daniel interpreted these four metals as symbolic of four successive empires that would rule over Israel—Babylon, Persia, Greece, and Rome. The feet, with ten toes, represented a final form of the Roman Empire in the end times, under the rule of ten leaders which I like to call the G-10. This has often been referred to as Rome II—a reunited, revived, reconstituted Roman Empire. Many believe the European Union is an embryonic phase of this final stage of the Roman Empire.

The main point, for our purposes, is that Daniel predicted the rise of the Persian Empire while Babylon was still ruling and accurately saw the future fall of Persia to Greece. This occurred two hundred years after Daniel died.

DANIEL 7: A LOPSIDED BEAR

Daniel 7 presents the same succession of empires as in Daniel 2, but in chapter 7, Daniel uses wild animals to symbolize the empires.

> I was looking in my vision by night, and behold, the four winds of heaven were stirring up the great sea. And four great beasts were coming up from the sea, different from one another. The first was like a lion and had the wings of an eagle. I kept looking until its wings were plucked, and it was lifted up from the ground and made to stand on two feet like a man; a human mind also was given to it. And behold, another beast, a second one, resembling a bear. And it was raised up on one side, and three ribs were in its mouth between its teeth; and thus they said to it, "Arise, devour much meat!" After this I kept looking, and behold, another one, like a leopard, which had on its back four wings of a bird; the beast also had four heads, and dominion was given to it. (Daniel 7:2–6)

The bear, which symbolizes the Medo-Persian Empire is pictured as lopsided because the Medians initially dominated the empire but were eventually superseded by the Persians. All this happened just as Daniel predicted.

DANIEL 8: A ROUTED RAM

The final prophecy about Persia that has already been fulfilled is found in Daniel 8.

> In the third year of the reign of Belshazzar the king a vision appeared to me, Daniel, subsequent to the one which appeared to me previously. I looked in the vision, and while I was looking I was in the citadel of

> Susa, which is in the province of Elam; and I looked in the vision and I myself was beside the Ulai Canal. Then I lifted my eyes and looked, and behold, a ram which had two horns was standing in front of the canal. Now the two horns were long, but one was longer than the other, with the longer one coming up last. I saw the ram butting westward, northward, and southward, and no other beasts could stand before him nor was there anyone to rescue from his power, but he did as he pleased and magnified himself. While I was observing, behold, a male goat was coming from the west over the surface of the whole earth without touching the ground; and the goat had a conspicuous horn between his eyes. He came up to the ram that had the two horns, which I had seen standing in front of the canal and rushed at him in his mighty wrath. I saw him come beside the ram, and he was enraged at him; and he struck the ram and shattered his two horns, and the ram had no strength to withstand him. So he hurled him to the ground and trampled on him, and there was none to rescue the ram from his power. (Daniel 8:1–7)

We are not left to our own imagination about the identity of the ram and the goat. Later in Daniel 8, the ram is identified as Persia and the goat as Greece (Daniel 8:20–21). This prophecy is amazingly specific. The ram has two horns. One is longer than the other, and the longer one came up last. The imagery is similar to the lopsided bear in Daniel 7. The goat in this prophecy overpowers the ram. The prophecy was fulfilled in the Medo-Persian Empire. The Medes, who were initially more powerful in the empire, were eclipsed by the Persians who became the dominant power. Eventually, Greece conquered both.

Daniel accurately predicted the details of the fall of the Persian Empire to Alexander the Great two hundred years before it happened in 334–331 B.C. After that crushing defeat, Persia never rose again in history to be a great power.

Daniel's Persian prophecies were fulfilled literally and historically with 100 percent accuracy. We can put them to the test like the hundreds of other biblical prophecies that have come to pass just as predicted.

ISAIAH: THE REIGN OF CYRUS THE GREAT

Daniel wasn't alone in prophesying about Persia. Almost two hundred years before Daniel prophesied, Isaiah uttered an astounding prophecy related to Persia and its greatest leader, King Cyrus. He is referred to in Isaiah 41:2–4, 25, but in Isaiah 44:28 and 45:1, he is specifically called by name more than one hundred years before he was born. Isaiah 45:2–6 goes even further, predicting Cyrus's conquests and his edicts allowing the Jewish people to return to their land.

Isaiah 44:28 specifically foretells Cyrus's restoration

of the Jews to their land and their temple worship. "It is I who says of Cyrus, 'He is my shepherd! And he will perform all My desire.' And he declares of Jerusalem, 'She will be built,' and of the temple, 'Your foundation will be laid.'" This was dramatically fulfilled in 2 Chronicles 36:22–23.

> Now in the first year of Cyrus king of Persia—in order to fulfill the word of the LORD by the mouth of Jeremiah—the LORD stirred up the spirit of Cyrus king of Persia, so that he sent a proclamation throughout his kingdom, and also put it in writing, saying, "Thus says Cyrus king of Persia, the LORD, the God of heaven, has given me all the kingdoms of the earth, and He has appointed me to build Him a house in Jerusalem, which is in Judah. Whoever is among you of all His people, may the LORD his God be with him, and let him go up!"

Interestingly, based on President Donald Trump's favorable treatment of Israel and the Jewish people, some have suggested he is a modern counterpart to Cyrus. There's no doubt President Trump has been a great friend and supporter of Israel. Every defender and friend of Israel owes the president thanks for his actions on behalf of the Jewish people and their homeland. His list of achievements is impressive.

President Trump moved the US embassy from Tel Aviv to Jerusalem (recognizing Jerusalem as Israel's capital), acknowledged the Golan Heights as part of Israel, legalized Jewish West Bank settlements, and signed an executive order that included condemnation of anti-Jewish bias as a form of discrimination. In his second presidency beginning in 2025, Trump took direct military action against Iran's nuclear program, ordering strikes on Iranian nuclear facilities that significantly damaged Iran's capabilities. Most recently, in October 2025, Trump successfully brokered the release of all remaining Israeli hostages held by Hamas and convened an international peace summit in Egypt, demonstrating his continued commitment to bringing stability to the Middle East.

In light of President Trump's actions and their similarity to those of Cyrus, some prophecy teachers have projected a prophetic link between these two leaders who are separated by more than twenty-five hundred years. During his first presidency, some noted that Cyrus is mentioned by name in Isaiah 45 and that Donald Trump was the forty-fifth president, suggesting divine design. Now serving as the forty-seventh president, such numerical speculation appears even more problematic. So, what should we make of this?

The connection between their actions toward Israel is certainly interesting. I have no problem seeing President Trump as similar to Cyrus in his favorable treatment of God's people. However, any prophetic linkage based on numerical coincidences is tenuous at best, and speculative and sensational at worst.

FROM PAST TO PRESENT

Ancient Persia passed off the world stage after being subjugated by the Greek Empire under Alexander the Great, just as Scripture predicted. After being absorbed by the Greeks, Persia ultimately faded and ended up on the ash heap of history as far as being a significant world player. That condition persisted for centuries, but in the last part of the twentieth century, we witnessed the newest incarnation of Imperial Iran as Iran ascended to a place of prominence in the Middle East under the rule of the ayatollah and radical Islam. Since that time, over four decades, Iran built itself into the major regional disruptor it became by 2023.

However, as we've seen, the events of 2023–2025 have fundamentally challenged Iran's regional ascendancy. The twelve-day Israel-Iran war of June 2025, combined with the collapse of Syria's Assad regime, the severe degradation of Hezbollah, and the weakening of Hamas, has dismantled much of Iran's carefully constructed "axis of resistance." These strategic defeats have left Iran more isolated and desperate than at any point since the 1979 revolution, yet still possessing its most dangerous capability: a nuclear program at the threshold of weapons production.

Iran's rise in recent decades is no accident, and neither is its current desperation. Both phases serve as key parts of the matrix of events setting the stage for the end times. Iran's modern trajectory—both its decades of regional expansion and its recent strategic collapse—aligns with the end-time prophecy found in Ezekiel 38–39. The fulfillment of this ancient prophecy requires not a triumphant Iran, but a desperate one: cornered, nuclear-armed, and driven to make the alliance with Russia and Turkey that the prophet foretold. Iran's current weakness may paradoxically accelerate, rather than prevent, the prophetic showdown Ezekiel described.

By June 2025, Iran had crossed every red line in nuclear development short of actually assembling a weapon. Intelligence agencies confirmed that Iran possessed over 408 kilograms of uranium enriched to 60 percent purity—a level that has no civilian application and is just steps away from the 90 percent needed for weapons. This represented a nearly 50 percent increase since February 2025 alone.

More alarming was Iran's breakout timeline. As we've noted, US intelligence assessed that Iran could now produce enough weapons-grade uranium for multiple nuclear devices in less than one week. The Defense Intelligence Agency confirmed Iran would need "probably less than one week" to produce sufficient fissile material for one nuclear weapon.

This threshold status triggered the dramatic events of June 2025—Israel's "preemptive" strikes against Iranian nuclear facilities at Fordow, Natanz, and Isfahan, while claiming that Iran was "closer than ever to obtaining a nuclear weapon." The strikes targeted not only enrichment facilities but also Iranian nuclear scientists and senior Revolutionary Guard commanders.

Iran responded with ballistic missile strikes on Israel,

escalating the conflict to unprecedented levels. The situation became even more critical when, on June 21–22, the United States launched its own military strikes against Iranian nuclear facilities. President Trump described the goal as to "destroy or severely degrade Iran's nuclear program."

The immediate damage assessment varied. While Trump claimed Iranian sites were "obliterated," intelligence reports suggested the setback might be measured in months rather than years. More significantly, Iranian Supreme Leader Khamenei announced that Iran would continue its nuclear program despite the attacks. Iran immediately began accelerating construction on a new underground facility at Kuh-e Kolang Gaz, potentially even deeper and more protected than previous sites.

A temporary ceasefire announced by President Trump on June 23, 2025, provided breathing room, but the fundamental dynamic remained unchanged. Iran's nuclear program had been damaged but not destroyed, and Iran's motivation to continue had only intensified. These final prophecies of Iran will be fulfilled just as literally and specifically as the ones in Isaiah and Daniel that have already happened.

The Bible is clear that Iran will be an integral part of a cluster of nations that will strike Israel in the end times. For the first time since Ezekiel penned his prophecy more than twenty-five hundred years ago, the necessary preconditions for its fulfillment are falling into place. The correlation between current events in Iran and the Middle East with Bible prophecy is striking.

THE ABRAHAM ACCORDS: A PROPHETIC REALIGNMENT

One of the most significant diplomatic developments in recent Middle East history has been the signing of the Abraham Accords beginning in September 2020. For the first time since Jordan made peace with Israel in 1994, Arab nations—the United Arab Emirates, Bahrain, Morocco, and Sudan—normalized relations with Israel. This represented a seismic shift away from the decades-old Arab League position that no Arab state would recognize Israel until Palestinian statehood was achieved.

The timing is prophetically significant. Ezekiel 38:11 describes Israel as "dwelling securely" when the great northern invasion occurs. The Abraham Accords have created unprecedented security partnerships between Israel and key Arab states. Israel now coordinates defense systems with the United Arab Emirates (UAE) and Bahrain, participates in joint naval exercises, and has established extensive trade relationships worth billions of dollars.

Even more remarkable is how these agreements have survived the challenges of recent conflicts. Despite the October 7, 2023 Hamas attacks and the subsequent Gaza war, none of the Abraham Accords signatories severed diplomatic ties with Israel. While public cooperation cooled during the height of the conflict, government-to-government relationships remained intact.

The Abraham Accords have also created what Israeli Prime Minister Netanyahu has termed an "Abraham

Alliance" against Iran. During Iran's missile attacks on Israel in 2024, Jordan, Saudi Arabia, and the UAE coordinated with Israeli and American forces to intercept Iranian projectiles. This cooperation against a common Iranian threat represents exactly the kind of regional realignment that sets the stage for Ezekiel's prophecy.

As of 2025, the Trump administration is actively working to expand the Abraham Accords to include Saudi Arabia, Syria, and Lebanon. Each new signatory further isolates Iran and strengthens the alliance that Iran views as an existential threat—potentially pushing Tehran toward the very coalition and actions that Ezekiel predicted 2,600 years ago. In fact, the prophetic timeline may be accelerating.

A TRIGGERING SHOCK

While Iran's nuclear program developed behind the scenes, the Middle East was shocked by events that began at dawn on October 7, 2023. Hamas launched an unprecedented, coordinated assault on Israel—the largest attack on Israeli territory since the 1948 Arab-Israeli War. Over 1,200 Israelis were killed, and 251 others were taken hostage to Gaza.

The attack's scale and brutality stunned the region. Hamas militants used rockets, paragliders, and ground infiltration to breach Israel's supposedly impregnable border defenses. The images of the massacre, many recorded by the attackers themselves, galvanized Israeli public opinion for a response that would dwarf any previous military action in Gaza.

What followed was Israel's longest war in its history. The ensuing conflict in Gaza has resulted in over 67,000 Palestinian casualties according to Gaza health authorities, the displacement of nearly the entire Gazan population, and the destruction of approximately 78 percent of Gaza's structures. A ceasefire finally took effect on October 10, 2025, involving hostage exchanges and partial Israeli withdrawal from Gaza cities.

From a prophetic perspective, October 7 accelerated every trend pointing toward Ezekiel 38. The attacks strengthened the Abraham Accords rather than destroying them. Despite initial strains, the UAE, Bahrain, and Morocco maintained diplomatic relations with Israel throughout the conflict. This demonstrated that the new Middle East alignments are more durable than traditional Arab solidarity with Palestinian causes.

Most significantly, the conflict has pushed both Israel and Iran toward positions that align perfectly with Ezekiel's prophecy. Israel, despite the ongoing war, continues to maintain security through its military superiority and alliance system. Iran, facing mounting pressure and proxy losses, grows more desperate and more likely to join the coalition that Ezekiel describes attacking from the north.

CHAPTER 5

THE ALIGNING OF NATIONS

In the thirty-eighth chapter of Ezekiel, it says that the land of Israel will come under attack by the armies of the ungodly nations . . . For the first time ever, everything is in place . . . It can't be too long now. Ezekiel says that fire and brimstone will be rained upon the enemies of God's people. That must mean that they will be destroyed by nuclear weapons.

—*President Ronald Reagan,* 1971

Theologians . . . studying the ancient prophecies . . . have said that never, in the time between the prophecies up until now, has there ever been a time in which so many of the prophecies are coming together. There have been times in the past when people thought the end of the world was coming, and so forth, but never anything like this.

—*President Ronald Reagan,* 1983

TWO DAYS BEFORE HE DIED ON THE CROSS, Jesus delivered one of His greatest sermons from the Mount of Olives, just east of Jerusalem, overlooking the Temple Mount. In that sermon known as the Olivet Discourse, Jesus outlined the signs that will portend His return to earth to deliver Jerusalem and judge the world.

In His discourse, Jesus uttered these sobering words, which have been repeated countless times across the centuries: "You will be hearing of wars and rumors of wars. See that you are not frightened, for those things must take place, but that is not yet the end. For nation will rise against nation, and kingdom against kingdom" (Matthew 24:6–7). According to Jesus, the end times will be marked by military conflict. They will be fraught with feuding and fighting. Peace will be removed from the earth and replaced with bloodshed (1 Thessalonians 5:1–3; Revelation 6:1–2).

Although the end times in general will be marred by wars and rumors of wars, two great conflicts will stand out from among the rest. The first is described by the Hebrew prophet Ezekiel in chapters 38–39 of the book named for him. (See the appendix, "The Great Showdown," to read these two chapters, to get the entire context of Ezekiel's prophecy.) These chapters describe a Russian-Islamic surprise attack on Israel that will threaten Israel's very existence. We'll discuss the details of this invasion in more detail in the next chapter.

The second great war of the end of days is the Battle

of Har-Magedon, or Armageddon, described in the book of Revelation:

> The sixth angel poured out his bowl on the great river, the Euphrates; and its water was dried up, so that the way would be prepared for the kings from the east. . . . And I saw . . . three unclean spirits . . . go out to the kings of the whole world, to gather them together for the war of the great day of God, the Almighty. ("Behold, I am coming like a thief. Blessed is the one who stays awake and keeps his clothes, so that he will not walk about naked and men will not see his shame.") And they gathered them together to the place which in Hebrew is called Har-Magedon. (16:12–16; cf. 14:19–20; 19:11–21)

Some scholars and biblical commentators maintain that Ezekiel 38 and Revelation 16 describe the same war. However, a careful reading of the two passages reveals that they depict two different conflicts separated by some span of time.

The war of Gog and Magog, in Ezekiel 38, will occur first and will involve a limited number of specifically named nations (vv. 1–6). The Battle of Armageddon will involve all the nations of the earth, will culminate in the Second Coming of Christ to earth, and will end the time of great Tribulation.

While the Battle of Armageddon must be years away, I believe the war of Gog and Magog could be on the near horizon. The dramatic events of 2023–2025 have accelerated the prophetic timeline: Israel's strikes on Iran's nuclear facilities, the fall of Assad's regime in Syria, the degradation of Hezbollah, and Iran's resulting desperation have created an unprecedented alignment of circumstances. The current showdown with Iran strikingly foreshadows this coming war. What we see happening today is the perfect buildup. The specific countries and circumstances are converging with accelerating speed to take their prophesied places just as we should expect if this war is coming.

In the popular movie *The Lord of the Rings: The Return of the King*, the wizard Gandalf gazes ahead to what's coming and says, "The board is set, the pieces are moving. . . . We come to it at last . . . the great battle of our time."[1] In a similar way, when we look at our world, we see that "the pieces are moving." The prophesied nations are aligning before our eyes. "The great battle of our time" may be fast approaching.

IRAN RISING

According to Ezekiel's prophecy Iran will be part of a colossal end-time strike force that will move into Israel. That much is certain. Persia, or modern Iran (the name was changed in 1935), is listed in Ezekiel 38:5 as one of the nations that will participate in this last-days invasion of Israel. That means the rise of Iran in the last forty years as the world's number one sponsor of terror and Israel's public enemy number one is no accident.

For Israel one thing is sure—Iran is coming. They won't miss the opportunity to try to wipe Israel off the map once and for all. As authors Charles Dyer and Mark Tobey wrote:

> Iran's hatred for Israel is a matter of religious conviction. They have invested uncounted billions in terror organizations and ever-more-deadly weapons of destruction, much of it intended to be used against Israel. Iran also knows its limitations and Israel's strengths, and that has kept it from pushing Israel too far. But if Iran were ever given an opportunity to be part of a massive coalition mobilizing against Israel, their leaders would jump at the chance.
>
> Ezekiel predicted that's exactly what they will do—when the time is right.[2]

But Iran won't come alone. Far from it. According to Ezekiel 38, a coalition of nations will join Iran's ill-fated invasion of Israel.

> And the word of the LORD came to me saying, "Son of man, set your face toward Gog of the land of Magog, the prince of Rosh, Meshech and Tubal, and prophesy against him and say, 'Thus says the Lord GOD, Behold, I am against you, O Gog, prince of Rosh, Meshech and Tubal. I will turn you about and put hooks into

> your jaws, and I will bring you out, and all your army, horses and horsemen, all of them splendidly attired, a great company with buckler and shield, all of them wielding swords; Persia, Ethiopia, and Put with them, all of them with shield and helmet; Gomer with all its troops; Beth-togarmah from the remote parts of the north with all its troops—many peoples with you.'" (vv. 1–6)

The coalition presented in these verses is already loosely in place and gathering momentum. Let's briefly examine the various nations that will be part of this strike force along with Iran.

THE MAN NAMED GOG

The first proper name in Ezekiel's list of enemies is "Gog," a word found eleven times in Ezekiel 38–39. The only other references to Gog are in 1 Chronicles 5:4, which has no connection with the Gog in Ezekiel 38, and in Revelation 20:8. *Gog* may mean "height" or "mountain," or alternatively it may be related to a word meaning "darkness." Whatever the precise meaning, this name points to a dark, menacing figure. Gog will be an enemy of God and Israel.

The context of Ezekiel reveals that Gog is an individual, not a nation, because he is personally addressed by God (38:14; 39:1) and is called a prince (38:2; 39:1).

Gog will be the commander of the anti-Israel coalition. Additionally, he is identified as the last-days leader of *Rosh*, which I believe refers to Russia (more about that later).

Many believe Gog is another title for the final Antichrist. I believe Gog and the Antichrist are two different end-time leaders of two separate coalitions of nations. Scripture presents the Antichrist as the head of a Western confederacy of nations sometimes called the reunited or revived Roman Empire, while, according to Ezekiel 38, Gog will preside over a Russian-Islamic bloc of nations. These men will rule over competing, opposing spheres vying for influence in the end of days.

I don't believe we should try to identify any modern leader as Gog or spend time trying to figure out the identity of the Antichrist. Trying to name the Antichrist is reckless and futile until the end times begin. In the same vein, there's no way to know for sure if the current leader of Russia is Gog. However, I find bestselling author Joel Rosenberg's words on Vladimir Putin insightful.

> Putin is a power-hungry, greedy, authoritarian, Czar wannabe. He is determined to expand Russian wealth, power and control over her neighbors. He has worked especially hard to build strategic alliances with Radical Islamic leaders and states in the Middle East. Over the years, people have asked me if Putin might be the Russian dictator referred to as "Gog" in the biblical prophecies of "Gog and Magog" in

> Ezekiel 38–39. . . . Here's my quick answer: It's too soon to draw such a conclusion. There's much more that would have to happen to indicate that Putin was the "Gog" of Bible prophecy. But there's no question in my mind that Putin is *Gog-esque.* He is dangerous, and both Israel and the West should keep a close and wary eye on him, especially given all that Putin has done to build a strategic alliance between Russia and Iran and the other countries mentioned in the "Gog and Magog" prophecies.[3]

At this point, it's impossible to say Putin is Gog or to conclusively say he is not. Time will tell. But I agree that at a minimum we can safely say Putin is *Gog-esque*. If nothing else, Putin serves as a forceful foreshadow of what Gog will be like when he does emerge on the world scene. Putin is a ruthless, shrewd leader who is galvanizing the Middle East under his umbrella of influence.

There is growing momentum in Russia among Putin's acolytes and many others to throw off term limits and for Putin to be the permanent leader of Russia—the czar. They want a return of the monarchy to Russia.[4] With the recent change to the Russian constitution, Putin is now eligible to maintain his grip on the presidency until 2036, but no one believes he will step down even then if he wants to continue. *The New York Times* calls him "Putin the Immortal." If not Putin, then another Russian leader like him will fulfill the Gog prophecy.

So, the first thing we discover about the rising Persian

Storm is that Iran will be allied with Russia. That's no stretch today, as Iran has dramatically deepened ties with Russia since 2022. Russia's invasion of Ukraine and subsequent Western sanctions have pushed both nations into a partnership of necessity. Iran has supplied Russia with thousands of drones for use against Ukraine, while Russia has provided Iran with advanced military technology and diplomatic cover. Iran has carried out naval war games with both Russia and China. This growing alliance perfectly mirrors the prophetic coalition described in Ezekiel. When Gog comes calling, Iran will jump at the chance to join the alliance to attack Israel and wipe them out once and for all.

THE GATHERING COALITION

According to Ezekiel, Gog will assemble a massive, multinational coalition. But as we read Ezekiel's prophecy, we need to recognize that none of the places mentioned in Ezekiel 38 can be found on any modern map. The only exception is the nation of Put, which some translate as Libya, which is known by the same name today. As we should expect, Ezekiel employed ancient place names that were familiar to the people of his day. The names of these geographical locations have changed numerous times through the millennia, and some could change again. Yet, the physical, geographical area remains the same. Whatever names these nations may bear at the time of this invasion, it's these geographical territories that will be involved. And they represent quite a diverse cast of characters.

MAGOG

Magog is the first of several ancient places listed by Ezekiel that are first mentioned in Genesis 10:2–4 in the Table of Nations. A fierce, warlike group of nomadic tribes known as the Scythians inhabited the land of Magog.[5] Their homeland spans from what today is known as central Asia across the southern steppes of modern Russia. Modern Magog includes many satellites of the former Soviet Union: Kazakhstan, Kirghizia, Uzbekistan, Turkmenistan, and Tajikistan. Putin has met with leaders of these nations to strategize and strengthen economic ties in light of increased sanctions that have throttled the Russian economy. Others maintain that Ukraine could be part of ancient Magog. Some believe Russia may be part of ancient Magog and that it could incorporate Afghanistan as well. With the exception of Russia, all these nations embrace Islam. Religion is the glue that will bring them together.

ROSH

Rosh is a reference to Russia. This connection is not based on the fact the two names sound alike. That's a poor argument for equating an ancient place with a modern nation. Compelling linguistic, historical evidence exists for making this connection.[6] More than two and a half millennia ago, the prophet Ezekiel predicted that in the latter times a people would invade Israel "from the distant north" or the "remotest parts of the north" (Ezekiel 38:6, 15 NLT; 39:2). Drawing a line up or north from Israel on any map leads directly to Russia. The Russian bear will be Israel's great nemesis from the north in the last days.

Since World War II, the mighty Russian bear has risen to a place of world power. When the Soviet Union was broken up in the early 1990s, many believed that the Russian bear was retreating into permanent hibernation. Of course, Russia lost territory and influence and was temporarily weakened and humiliated. But under the leadership of Vladimir Putin, the Russian bear has come roaring back and is a much more dangerous bear than ever before. Russia has more nuclear warheads today than any nation on earth. Putin wants to lead Russia back to its former days of glory. In a speech at the Kremlin, Putin referred to the collapse of the Soviet Union as " the greatest geopolitical disaster of the century."[7] Implicit within that statement is that the greatest achievement of the century would be the Soviet Union's restoration. Putin longs to restore the glory days of the Soviet Empire.

The preparatory buildup for the Gog invasion seems to be developing right before our eyes. For the first time in history Russia and Iran are allies, working together to exert influence over the Middle East. Ezekiel 38 could never have been fulfilled until the last few years. Daily headlines bear a remarkable correspondence to Ezekiel's prophecy, written more than five hundred years before the birth of Christ. This is strong support for the inspiration of the Bible. Only God can predict the future with pinpoint accuracy.

Any day now, Israel may resume their war that ended in June 2025. Both Iran and Israel believe they have unfinished business—with Iran harboring an insatiable desire for revenge. Israel, aided by the US, may initiate another conflict with Iran if there's any notion that Iran has restarted its nuclear program. It wants to make sure Iran's nuclear program is inoperative or nonexistent. But the first missile in a resumed war could be launched by Iran. The Iranian mullahs want to forever eliminate the "Zionist cancer." When war inevitably breaks out again, no matter who fires the first shot, Iran will seek revenge at all cost. Payback will be palpable. The next conflict could function as the lighting of the fuse that precipitates the gathering of the Ezekiel 38 alliance.

Ezekiel 38 pictures Russia as reluctant to lead the invasion of Israel in the end times. The prophet refers to the "hooks" in the "jaws" that God will use to pull Russia into this foray (v. 4). Pressure from Iran to punish Israel for an attack could be the force that's needed to draw Russia in. Russia has a vital stake in Iran. Its deepening connection to Iran could eventually force its hand, pulling it into leading the invasion of Israel.

MESHECH AND TUBAL

Meshech and Tubal normally appear together in Scripture. They are mentioned two other times in Ezekiel

(27:13; 32:26). Meshech and Tubal are the ancient *Moschoi* and *Tibarenoi* in Greek writings. They are the *Tabal* and *Musku* in Assyrian inscriptions. These ancient nations are located in what today is Turkey.

ETHIOPIA (CUSH)

The Hebrew word *Cush* in Ezekiel 38:5 is frequently translated "Ethiopia" in modern English versions. In ancient times Cush was known as *Kusu* by the Assyrians and Babylonians, *Kos* or *Kas* by the Egyptians, and *Nubia* by the Greeks. Cush was consistently located directly south of ancient Egypt in what today is Sudan.

Russia's activity in Sudan is deeper than ever before. Sudan also maintains a strong partnership with Turkey. The Islamic nation is now free of any influence from the Christian south and is at liberty to act on its own. Sudan is a zealous Islamic stronghold that supported Iraq in the Gulf War and sheltered Osama bin Laden for five years in the 1990s. It stands ready to take its place in the coming Gog alliance against Israel just as Ezekiel predicted. Sudan has recently offered Russia its first coveted naval base in Africa for twenty-five years in exchange for arms.

LIBYA (PUT)

The Hebrew word *Put* or *Phut* is found in Ezekiel 38:5. The Septuagint, which was the Greek translation of the Old Testament, translates the word as *Libues*. For this reason, several modern translations, including the King James Version, the New King James Version, and the New Living Translation, substitute the word *Libya* in this verse. Ancient sources locate Put in North Africa to the west of Egypt. The nation immediately west of Egypt is Libya, but Put could include nations even farther west, such as Algeria and Tunisia.

Modern Libya was ruled by Colonel Muammar al-Qaddafi from 1969 until the outbreak of the revolution in 2011 during the Arab Spring, when he was violently killed. In the aftermath, Libya descended into the chaos of civil war in 2014 that was finally ended by a cease-fire in 2020. However, rival factions are still dueling for power in a bloody civil conflict.

Turkey has supported one side in the ongoing clash and is deepening bilateral ties with Libya. As Russia's presence in Syria has diminished after the fall of the dynasty of Basher Al-Assad, its influence in Libya has dramatically increased. Russia is scrambling to shift resources to Libya. The Heritage Foundation has sounded the alarm about Russia's push for power in Libya.[8] Moscow has assumed a growing role in Libya's war. These deepening connections with Turkey and Russia will prove instrumental in drawing Libya into the Gog coalition to invade Israel when the time comes.

GOMER

While some prophecy teachers erroneously equate Gomer with modern-day Germany, Gomer represents the ancient Cimmerians, or *Kimmerioi*. According to ancient sources Gomer is associated with the Akkadian *Gi-mir-ra-a* and the Armenian *Gamir*. From the eighth century

B.C., the Cimmerians occupied territory in Anatolia, which makes up the majority of modern Turkey. The Jewish historian Josephus stated that the Gomerites were equated with the Galatians, who inhabited central Turkey.[9]

BETH-TOGARMAH

Beth-Togarmah means the "house of Togarmah." The ancient Assyrians referred to Togarmah as *Til-garamu*, while the Hittites used the word *Tegarma*. Either way, the territory of Togarmah is located in modern Turkey, which is north of Israel.

As you can see, four of the names in Ezekiel 38:1–6 refer to Turkey—Meshech, Tubal, Gomer, and Beth-Togaramah. Turkey is an ally of Iran and an avowed enemy of Israel. Under Recep Tayyip Erdoğan, who assumed the Turkish presidency in 2003, Turkey has taken a strong turn toward dictatorship and an adamantly anti-Israel posture. His opposition toward Israel is straightforward: "Whoever is on the side of Israel, let everyone know that we are against them."[10] He never misses an opportunity to castigate and condemn Israel.

Erdoğan champions the cause of the Palestinians, denounces Israel at every turn, and even repeatedly calls Hamas a "resistance movement." He supported President Trump's Gaza Peace Plan, but it appears his support was carefully calculated to increase Turkey's influence in the region to further his goal of a new Ottoman Empire. Erdoğan "hopes the deal can pave the way for more Turkish influence in Gaza and around the region."[11]

As Iran and Russia have largely lost influence in Syria due to their growing headaches on their own home fronts, Turkey has moved in to expand its sway in Syria which is poised right on Israel's northern border.

The prominence of Turkey in Ezekiel 38 also highlights an interesting twist. The Quran contains its own version of the Battle of Gog and Magog, which it calls the War of Yajuj and Majuj (18:96; 21:96) and which involves Turkey. The Quranic version was written about a thousand years after Ezekiel prophesied and teaches that Gog and Magog were two bands of Turks that spread corruption through the earth during the time of Abraham. They were eventually imprisoned behind a great barrier to restrain their activity. Throughout the centuries they tried to escape without success. When Allah issues his decree in the end times, the barrier will collapse, and Gog and Magog will rush out in all directions, pouring into the land of Israel to attack Muslims living there. Allah will wipe them out in response to the prayers of Jesus, using a terrible, deadly disease or plague. This language was clearly borrowed from Ezekiel 38:22, and adapted to fit a totally different narrative and outcome.

THE END-TIME COALITION AGAINST ISRAEL

The nations in this list are all enemies or at least not friends with Israel. They all have the desire at one level or another to get rid of Israel. To varying degrees, they are either forming or strengthening their ties to one another. They all appear regularly in the headlines, some almost every day. No great leap is necessary to imagine these nations colluding together to overrun Israel in the near future, especially if Israel's running feud with Iran explodes.

Rosh (ancient Rashu, Rasapu, Ros, and Rus)	Russia
Magog (ancient Scythians)	Central Asia
Meshech (ancient Muschki and Musku)	Turkey
Tubal (ancient Tubalu)	Turkey
Persia	Iran
Ethiopia (Cush)	Sudan
Put or Phut	Libya
Gomer (ancient Cimmerians)	Turkey
Beth-togarmah (ancient Til-garimmu or Tegarma)	Turkey

Ezekiel's list of the nations in this last-days invasion ends with these words: "many peoples with you" (Ezekiel 38:6). This catch-all phrase could indicate that more nations, not specifically listed, will join the war against Israel. Ezekiel lists Israel's distant or far enemies in every direction. North is Russia, east is Iran, south is Sudan, and west is Libya. By listing these far enemies, Ezekiel may be including the inner ring of nations around Israel as well, nations or territories such as Syria, Jordan, Egypt, Lebanon, Iraq, and Gaza. It could also include more distant nations as well. Russia has consigned thousands of foreign troops in its war with Ukraine from Nepal, North Korea, and even a large contingent from Cuba.

Whatever measure you use, the ingredients for the Gog coalition seem to be coming together. All that's required to finish the process is a catalyst. The showdown between Iran and Israel could easily be the trigger that sets the final movements in motion.

THE OPPOSITION

Everything we see today suggests that Iran and the other nations in Ezekiel 38 are on a collision course with Israel and would gladly join the Gog alliance when it comes together.

Nevertheless, the Middle East is a complicated place. Iran has many enemies, even among Muslims, who fear her and would do anything to neutralize her power and influence. In the current climate, we would expect many nations to avoid any Iranian war with Israel and even root for an Iranian defeat.

Ezekiel 38 corresponds to what we see today, both in the nations that are part of the coalition against Israel as well as those who oppose it. The specificity of this prophecy is astounding. Ezekiel presents the nations in the Gog coalition that will join Russia and Iran against Israel and also lays out the nations that will object to the invasion, albeit lamely. Amazingly, this assembly of nations that sits on the sidelines and lodges its protest is just as perfectly aligned as the aggressors.

> Thus says the Lord GOD, "It will come about on that day, that thoughts will come into your mind and you will devise an evil plan, and you will say, 'I will go up against the land of unwalled villages. I will go against those who are at rest, that live securely, all of them living without walls and having no bars or gates, to capture spoil and to seize plunder, to turn your hand against the waste places which are *now* inhabited, and against the people who are gathered from the nations, who have acquired cattle and goods, who live at the center of the world.' Sheba and Dedan and the merchants of Tarshish with all its villages will say to you, 'Have you come to capture spoil? Have you assembled your company to seize plunder, to carry away silver and gold, to take away cattle and goods, to capture great spoil?'" (Ezekiel 38:10–13)

Who are the nations who lodge their protest to the Iranian invasion of Israel?

SHEBA AND DEDAN

The first protesting nations are identified as "Sheba and Dedan and the merchants of Tarshish with all its villages." Sheba and Dedan are easy to locate. They're the nations we know today as Saudi Arabia and the more moderate Gulf States such as Qatar and the UAE. The UAE and Bahrain have signed on to the Abraham Accords that normalized relations with Israel. These Muslim nations are vehemently opposed to Iran and its nuclear quest. Bahrain severed relations with Iran in 2016.

What we see today lines up seamlessly with Ezekiel's prophecy. It requires no active imagination to envision these nations opposing Iran's actions, yet standing on the sidelines, taking a knee, and offering no more than verbal dissent when the Gog invasion erupts.

MERCHANTS OF TARSHISH

The reference to "the merchants of Tarshish with all its villages" (Ezekiel 38:13) poses a greater challenge to identify. Even English translations differ somewhat.

English Standard Version	"the merchants of Tarshish and all its leaders"
King James Version	"the merchants of Tarshish, with all the young lions thereof"
New Living Translation	"the merchants of Tarshish"
New International Version	"the merchants of Tarshish and all her villages"

Three ancient locations were identified as "Tarshish."[12] The most accepted view is that Tarshish was a wealthy, flourishing Phoenician colony situated in modern Spain.

This outpost was renowned for exporting silver, iron, tin, and lead (Jeremiah 10:9; Ezekiel 27:12, 25).

The words "and all its leaders" (ESV) or "the young lions thereof" (KJV) seem to refer to powerful, energetic rulers who will join with Tarshish to verbally oppose Gog's invasion. These leaders will evidently walk in lockstep with Tarshish. Tarshish is often associated in Scripture with the far West. When the prophet Jonah wanted to go as far away from Nineveh as possible, he headed to Tarshish (Jonah 1:1–3). Since Tarshish, located in Spain, was the farthest western location known in that day, I believe "Tarshish and all its leaders" is a reference to the Western powers or Western world in the end times who will join the moderate Arab states in denouncing the invasion of Israel.[13]

The mention of Western powers brings up the possibility the United States is included in this group of protesting nations. While there's no way to make this connection with any certainty, it remains a realistic possibility. Nevertheless, even if this is a veiled reference to America, it provides almost no helpful insight into any activities by the United States other than a weak protest against the Russian-Islamic invasion of Israel. So, either way, it's not really significant. We'll discuss possible biblical identifications of the United States further in chapter 8.

INTENSIFYING INTERSECTION

As you can see, the scenario presented in Ezekiel 38 mirrors the present world political situation. The current

Russia-Iran alliance has deepened significantly amid both nations' isolation from the West. Russia's invasion of Ukraine in 2022 and subsequent international sanctions have pushed Moscow closer to Tehran, creating a partnership of necessity that mirrors the prophetic alliance described in Ezekiel. Iran has supplied Russia with drones and military equipment for use in Ukraine, while Russia has provided Iran with advanced military technology and diplomatic cover.[14]

Russia continues to expand its footprint in the Middle East, forging and fortifying partnerships with Iran, Turkey, and other nations. Turkey's position in this prophetic scenario has become increasingly complex. While Turkey maintains its NATO membership, President Erdoğan has cultivated closer ties with both Russia and Iran, particularly regarding regional energy projects and opposition to Israeli policies. This triangular relationship between Turkey, Russia, and Iran creates the exact configuration anticipated in Ezekiel's prophecy.[15]

The Islamic nations that correspond to ancient Magog (central Asia) are developing and deepening ties with Iran, Russia, and Turkey. Hatred for Israel in Iran and other Muslim nations in the region continues to seethe. It's easy to picture the alliance Ezekiel describes pouring into Israel in an all-out attempt to wipe Israel off the face of the earth. Likewise, in the current climate, it's not too difficult to imagine the moderate Gulf States and Western democracies raising loud protest and objection to the invasion but opting to stand on the sidelines and watch the whole matter unfold.

Ezekiel's prophecy reads like today's headlines. The dramatic events of 2023–2025 have accelerated the prophetic timeline: Israel's preemptive strikes on Iran's nuclear facilities, the degradation of Hezbollah's capabilities, the fall of Assad's regime in Syria, and Iran's consequent desperation have created an unprecedented alignment of circumstances. While Iran has suffered significant setbacks, these very defeats may drive the regime toward the desperate alliance and invasion described in Ezekiel 38–39.[16]

Again, remember that Iran's recent military humiliations have not eliminated the threat but may have intensified it. A cornered and weakened Iran, having lost key proxies and facing internal pressure, may be more likely to risk everything in a final gambit. The regime's survival instincts, combined with their eschatological beliefs about hastening the return of the Twelfth Imam through chaos and war, create a dangerous dynamic that aligns perfectly with Ezekiel's description of a desperate invasion attempt.[17]

We can't be sure what the trigger will be, but the gathering storm with Iran is looking more and more likely as a candidate. I appreciate Joel Rosenberg's admonition in light of Ezekiel 38–39:

> What then are we to make of all this? It is almost as if the Lord has perfectly allowed world circumstances to

conform in more than one way, giving us multiple possibilities to fulfill Ezekiel's prophecy. Is Gog emerging in front of us? We may find out very soon. One thing is clear however; the Lord wants us all to remain alert and on our knees.[18]

Amen!

CHAPTER 6

THE GATHERING STORM: THE WAR OF GOG AND MAGOG

> This war will be a war unlike any we have seen thus far in history.
>
> —*Dr. Walter C. Kaiser Jr., Preaching and Teaching the Last Things*

IN 2019 MY WIFE AND I and another couple had the privilege of visiting Normandy, France, on June 5, the day before the seventy-fifth anniversary of the D-Day invasion. We hired a van and a driver for the day and drove up from Paris. The entire region was filled with reenactors dressed in uniforms from World War II. Tanks, trucks, jeeps, and cannons were on display everywhere. World War II–era airplanes were humming overhead. We made several stops in the area, but the most important, moving site was Omaha Beach. The Normandy American Cemetery and Memorial is located on a beautiful bluff overlooking Omaha Beach. Almost ten thousand crosses line the landscape.

The most special aspect of the trip was seeing the aged veterans who had taken part in the invasion return for one final act of remembrance. I'll never forget meeting them and hearing their harrowing stories. They were applauded everywhere they went and received much deserved appreciation. Waiting in the airport for our return home from Paris, my wife and I sat next to two venerable gentlemen who had hit the beaches to free a continent. On our flight home, another survivor of the Normandy invasion sat across us. Spending time with these heroes was better than any history lesson one could imagine.

The invasion in June 1944 was officially known as Operation Overlord, but the popular name is D-Day. According to CNN, "The 'D' stands for Day. D-Day is code for the day an important military attack is scheduled to begin."[1]

After a great deal of strategizing and planning, D-Day was finally scheduled by General Dwight Eisenhower for June 6, 1944. As we've seen, God has a D-Day scheduled on His prophetic calendar—a day when an important military attack will begin that will ultimately bring great victory and triumph for God and His people. This end-time D-Day is the Battle of Gog and Magog. The key actors are moving into place for its commencement. Chief among them is Iran.

But what will happen on this D-Day when Iran and its allies launch their all-out invasion of Israel? How will the showdown with Iran culminate? Where's it all headed? Ezekiel graphically describes what happens before, during, and after the battle.

BEFORE THE BATTLE: THE AIM

While many of the details of the final showdown with Iran are shrouded in mystery, the one thing we can know for sure is that this invasion will occur. It's already scheduled on God's prophetic calendar. While there's much we can't know, we do know the nations that will join this invasion. Ezekiel specifically identifies them, as we've already seen.

Ezekiel also provides some of the reasons or motivations for this attack. He clearly states their aim in their aggression against Israel. Several reasons for this invasion can be discerned from the text and related passages.

TO CAPTURE THE WEALTH OF ISRAEL

The exact nature of the wealth in Ezekiel 38:11–12 is never specifically stated; however, recent discoveries of vast oil and gas reserves in Israel are one possible answer. Several gargantuan natural gas deposits and shale oil sites have been discovered in various locations.

TO COMMAND THE MIDDLE EAST

Taking out Israel would give Iran and the other Islamic nations their greatest victory and prize and pave the way for their long past empire to be reestablished.

TO CONQUER ISRAEL

Every Muslim nation covets the reality of driving Israel into the sea. Ezekiel says these invaders will "come like a storm" and "like a cloud covering the land" (38:9). This sounds like a desire to overwhelm and overrun Israel, leaving nothing behind but ruin.

TO CONTEST THE ANTICHRIST

Assuming this invasion occurs during the first half of the coming seven-year Tribulation, as I believe, Israel will be enjoying her peace treaty with Antichrist when this attack occurs. This seven-year agreement is highlighted in Daniel 9:27. It tells us that the Antichrist, the leader of the Western confederacy in the end times, will broker a peace deal with Israel that will give them sovereignty over the Temple Mount. Daniel 9:27 says "he" (the coming prince the previous verse) will make a "firm" covenant with the many in Israel. The Hebrew *gabar*, often translated "firm" or "strong," can refer to a strong or even compelled covenant, meaning that the Antichrist may force the parties to the peace table with a "take it or take it" deal. But it can also mean the Antichrist will strengthen or "make strong" a covenant that already exists. This makes sense considering the Abraham Accord and other peace deals that are either in place or on the horizon. The Antichrist may rise on the world stage by strengthening a peace framework or template that's already in place.

With this peace agreement in place between the Antichrist and Israel, an attack against Israel would at the same time represent a direct confrontation against the

Antichrist. The invasion of Israel will be an open challenge to the West and its leader, the Antichrist, by Russia and its Islamic allies. Parallel prophecies in Daniel 9:27 and 11:41–44 tell us that at the midpoint of the seven-year Tribulation, the Antichrist will break his covenant with Israel and invade the land himself. Obviously, the total annihilation of the Russian-Islamic forces will leave a gaping power vacuum. The Antichrist will seize this opportunity to fill that void and consolidate his power. This will lead to the establishment of his one world religion, government, and economy, which will dominate the world for the final three and a half years of the end times, just before the return of Christ.

TO COUNTER THE REBUILDING OF THE JEWISH TEMPLE

During the first half of the seven-year Tribulation, Israel will rebuild its temple (Daniel 9:27; Matthew 24:15; 2 Thessalonians 2:4). It could be that Iran and these allies invade Israel to protect the Dome of the Rock and the Al-Aqsa mosque that stand on the Temple Mount. The entire thirty-six-acre area that the Jews call the Temple Mount is known by Muslims as al-Haram ash-Sharif, or the Noble Sanctuary. Any attempt by the Jewish people to rebuild their temple could set off this furious attack by the Muslim world supported by Russia.

DURING THE BATTLE: THE AVALANCHE

After the preparations for the battle are completed, the enemy armies will swoop into the unsuspecting nation of

Israel living in peace and prosperity. Ezekiel describes the invading flood in vivid terms, saying the armies will come "like a storm and cover the land like a cloud" (38:9). The battle and its outcome are presented in devastating detail.

When these nations invade the land of Israel, it will look like the most one-sided mismatch in history. The odds will be overwhelmingly in favor of the invaders. The world will look on in stunned fear as it appears Israel is about to be annihilated. The armies will gather and pour into the land like an invading swarm of locusts. From all appearances, Israel is finished. But just when it looks as though all is lost, God will dramatically intervene on behalf of Israel. He will descend in His fury to destroy the would-be conquerors: "But this is what the Sovereign LORD says: When Gog invades the land of Israel, my fury will boil over!" (Ezekiel 38:18 NLT).

The Battle of Gog and Magog will be the greatest turnaround in history. The tables will turn in a flash—from Israel's certain destruction to absolute triumph. God will come down to deliver Israel. Dr. Walter Kaiser Jr., quoted at the beginning of this chapter, says that "God, for his own name's sake, will sensationally rescue Israel when all other sources of help fail."[2]

Of course, God could just speak the word and the armies would melt before Him, but in this battle, He will employ four disasters to destroy the invading horde.

1. A DEVASTATING EARTHQUAKE (EZEKIEL 38:19–20)

The earthquake will be cataclysmic.

> "In My zeal and in My blazing wrath I declare that on that day there will surely be a great earthquake in the land of Israel. The fish of the sea, the birds of the heavens, the beasts of the field, all the creeping things that creep on the earth, and all the men who are on the face of the earth will shake at My presence; the mountains also will be thrown down, the steep pathways will collapse and every wall will fall to the ground."

2. DEADLY INFIGHTING AMONG THE INVADING ARMY (38:21)

In the chaos that ensues from the rattling earthquake, the invasion force will be thrown into confusion and will turn against itself. The soldiers will kill anyone in sight. When the dust settles, this will be the biggest incident of death by friendly fire in military history.

3. DREADFUL DISEASE (38:22)

An outbreak of incurable, lethal plagues will kill people instantly.

4. DRIVING RAIN, HAILSTONES, FIRE, AND BURNING SULFUR (38:22)

The Battle of Gog and Magog won't last long. When God steps in, the destruction will be swift and sobering. Smoldering heaps of weapons will litter the land. Carnage will cover the country.

Dr. Walter Kaiser summarizes the catastrophic defeat:

> But things will not end well for the nations that press their attack against Israel, for in the end, what they

> are doing is nothing less than an attack on God and his plan for time and eternity. In one great push, an axis of nations from that part of the world will make one huge incursion into the land of Israel, but that will call for the response of God himself. The carnage, bloodshed and loss of life and power will be unrivaled up to that point in history. This will be at once one of the darkest, and yet also one of the brightest, days of all history, as God settles the issue in a startling way. Such is the predicted fortunes of the War of Gog and Magog against Israel in the end of the days of history's ongoing time line.[3]

COLLATERAL DAMAGE

As crushing as the defeat will be for the invaders, it won't end in the land of Israel. Ezekiel says that the firestorms of God's judgment will extend even to the homeland of some of the invading nations. "And I will send fire upon Magog and those who inhabit the coastlands in safety; and they will know that I am the LORD" (Ezekiel 39:6).

Commenting on this verse, Joel Rosenberg said:

> This suggests that targets throughout Russia and the former Soviet Union, as well as Russia's allies, will be supernaturally struck on this day of judgment and partially or completely consumed. These could be limited to nuclear missile silos, military bases, radar installations, defense ministries, intelligence

> headquarters, and other government buildings of various kinds. But such targets could very well also include religious centers, such as mosques, madrassas, Islamic schools and universities, and other facilities that preach hatred against Jews and Christians and call for the destruction of Israel. Either way, we will have to expect extensive collateral damage, and many civilians will be at severe risk.[4]

The extent of this collateral damage is not stated, but we can be sure it will send a strong message of God's displeasure with the actions of these nations as well as evidence of His sovereign might.

CHRONOLOGICAL DECISION

One principal issue about this coming war is its timing. When does this invasion fit on God's prophetic calendar? The chronology of this invasion has been related to about every point in the end times. Some believe it could transpire at any time, and that the invasion will precede the rapture or at least the Tribulation.[5] Others believe Ezekiel 38 is another description of the final Battle of Armageddon.[6] Still others equate it with the reference to Gog and Magog in Revelation 20:8.[7]

In an effort not to get too far in the weeds, I won't present the pros and cons of all the views in detail, but I do want to briefly consider several internal markers that help us locate this invasion on the end-time schedule of events.

First, the Jewish people must be regathered to their ancient homeland. Ezekiel 37 is the prophetic prelude to the invasion in Ezekiel 38, and it prophesies the end-time regathering of the Jewish people to the land of Israel. Clearly the Jewish people in the nation of Israel cannot be invaded if the nation doesn't exist. The regathering and restoration of the Jewish people beginning in the 1940s was a key event that set many other prophecies in motion. As John Walvoord noted, "Ezekiel's prophecy obviously could not have been fulfilled prior to 1945, for the nation of Israel was not regathered to her ancient land. Until recently Israel's situation did not correspond to that which is described in Ezekiel's passage. Ezekiel's prophecy of twenty-five hundred years ago seems to have anticipated the return of Israel to their ancient land as a prelude to the climax of the present age."[8] Israel's presence in the land is the first major precondition that must be in place for this war to begin.

Second, the invasion will happen in the "last days" or "latter years" of Israel's history. This narrows the timing and setting of the invasion to the end times, but more specifically after the rapture of the church to heaven. Only then will the latter years for Israel begin.

Third, Ezekiel prophesies that Iran and her allies will come against Israel "after many days" at a time when the people of Israel are living in relative peace and prosperity (38:8–12). Ezekiel repeatedly emphasizes that when this invasion occurs, Israel will be back in the land, "living securely" (38:8,11,14) and "at rest" (38:11). Despite what some believe, this hardly describes what we see in Israel today. The land is prosperous but not at peace or at rest. Israelis live in a constant state of high alert. But according to Scripture, a time is coming when Israel will enjoy a season of peace and let down its guard. This will come about when Israel enters into a covenant or treaty with the coming Western leader, who will be the final Antichrist (Daniel 9:27). Under this treaty he will guarantee Israel peace and security. Therefore, for this invasion to occur, Israel must be present in the land, prosperous, and peaceful.

Taking all these internal markers into consideration, I believe this battle will occur during the first half of the coming seven-year Tribulation, possibly early in that window of time, when Israel will be living under her peace treaty with Antichrist. Pastor and evangelical author David Jeremiah agrees: "Thus, we have the time of the . . . invasion of Israel pinpointed. To summarize, it will come after Israel returns to this homeland, after it has become highly prosperous, and after the implementation of the seven-year peace treaty with the Antichrist."[9]

The late John Walvoord held the same view of the timing of this battle. "There is only one period in the future that clearly fits this description of Ezekiel," he wrote, "and that is the first half of Daniel's seventieth week of God's program for Israel (Daniel 9:27)."[10] He continues: "Under that covenant, Israel will be able to relax, for their Gentile enemies will have become their friends, apparently guaranteeing their borders and promising them freedom. During that first three and one-half years, we have the one time when regathered Israel is at rest and secure."[11]

The buildup we see today indicates that the coming of Christ to rapture His people to heaven could be very soon, setting in motion the cascade of events that will bring about the Battle of Gog and Magog.

THE BATTLE'S AFTERMATH

Three main events unfold in the aftermath of the battle.

1. THE CALL TO THE FEAST (EZEKIEL 39:4–5, 17–20)

The aftermath of the battle is a grisly, gruesome scene. The carnage that results from this slaughter will provide a great feast for the birds of the air and the beasts of the field. God refers to the carnage as His "sacrificial feast" (39:17 ESV) and His "banquet table" (39:20 NLT), to which He invites the birds and the beasts as His guests.

> "As for you, son of man, thus says the Lord God, 'Speak to every kind of bird and to every beast of the field, "Assemble and come, gather from every side to My sacrifice which I am going to sacrifice for you, as a great sacrifice on the mountains of Israel, that you may eat flesh and drink blood. You will eat the flesh of mighty men and drink the blood of the princes of the earth, as though they were rams, lambs, goats and

> bulls, all of them fatlings of Bashan. So you will eat fat until you are glutted, and drink blood until you are drunk, from My sacrifice which I have sacrificed for you. You will be glutted at My table with horses and charioteers, with mighty men and all the men of war," declares the Lord God. (Ezekiel 39:17–20)

A similar banquet will be held after the Battle of Armageddon at the end of the Tribulation (Revelation 19:17–21).

2. THE CLEANSING OF THE LAND (EZEKIEL 39:11–12, 14–16)

The cleansing of the land entails two stages. First, sanitation squads will comb the countryside for seven months after the battle. Not all the bodies can be buried quickly, and the bones will be left behind. These clean-up teams will set up markers wherever they see a human bone. The gravediggers coming behind them will see the markers and remove the remains to the valley of Hamon-Gog, which means "Gog's hordes," for burial. The cleansing efforts will be so widespread that a town will be constructed in the valley near the gravesites to aid those who are cleansing the land. The name of the town will be *Hamonah* (horde). Concerning the burial of these invading armies, Warren Wiersbe said, "They arrogantly entered Israel as proud soldiers but would be buried like slaughtered animals."[12]

The second phase of cleansing the land will involve burning the leftover weapons for seven years (Ezekiel

39:9–10). In describing the weapons used during this invasion, Ezekiel refers to "shields and bucklers, bows and arrows, war clubs and spears" (39:9). Ezekiel mentions horses as the means of transportation for the invading army (38:4, 15). Some believe the devastation during the future time of Tribulation, possibly from the use of nuclear weapons, will be so severe that armies will regress to using ancient weapons and riding on horses. There are faint indications that this could be realized in the future. In early 2025, *Forbes* ran this headline: "After Losing 15,000 Vehicles, Some Russian Troops In Ukraine Are Riding Horses." The article says, "It's finally happened. A video that circulated on social media this week depicts two Russian soldiers riding horses across the muddy Ukrainian landscape. Russian mechanized regiments have been losing armored vehicles at an annualized rate of 6,000 a year."[13]

"Russian assault troops fighting in Ukraine may soon find themselves on horseback. According to the newspaper *Kommersant*, the Russian army is attempting to revive full-fledged cavalry units."[14]

It is said that in 1947 Albert Einstein was asked at a dinner party what new weapons he believed might be employed in World War III. After a long pause, he allegedly responded, "I don't know what weapons might be used in World War III. But there isn't any doubt what weapons will be used in World War IV . . . stone spears."[15]

While that scenario is certainly possible, I believe it's probably best to understand Ezekiel's language as referring to contemporary equivalents such as tanks, rifles, modern artillery, drones, and missiles. Otherwise it would have had no meaning for the people living in Ezekiel's day. The recent Iran-Russia partnership demonstrates exactly this kind of modern warfare: Iran supplies Russia with Shahed drones for use in Ukraine, while Russia provides Iran with advanced missile technology. We should view these weapons the same way we interpret the nations in Ezekiel 38. We look for the modern counterparts of Rosh, Gomer, Persia, and so on, since the ancient names are no longer relevant.

Since the Battle of Gog and Magog occurs during the first half of the Tribulation, the Israelites will continue to burn these weapons for the remainder of the seven-year Tribulation and for a brief time on into the millennial kingdom that will follow as the land is cleansed and purified.

3. THE CONFIRMATION OF THE LORD (EZEKIEL 39:6–7)

As He unleashes His wrath and fury, God will graciously pour out His mercy. He will use the awesome display of His holiness and greatness against the invading armies not only to protect His people but also to bring many to salvation, both from the nations and from Israel.

> "I will bring you against My land, so that the nations may know Me when I am sanctified through you before their eyes, O Gog. . . . I will magnify Myself, sanctify Myself, and make Myself known in the sight

> of many nations; and they will know that I am the LORD. . . . And I will send fire upon Magog and those who inhabit the coastlands in safety; and they will know that I am the LORD. My holy name I will make known in the midst of My people Israel; and I will not let My holy name be profaned anymore. And the nations will know that I am the LORD, the Holy One in Israel. . . . And I will set My glory among the nations. . . . And the house of Israel will know that I am the LORD their God from that day onward." (Ezekiel 38:16, 23; 39:6, 7, 21, 22)

Charles Ryrie, in *The Ryrie Study Bible*, notes, "The twofold purpose of this judgment is that the nations might acknowledge God's glory and that Israel might know God's grace."[16]

It's often true that times of disaster and even judgment can bring people to their senses. Judgment serves as a sobering wake-up call. While I don't believe 9/11 was necessarily an act of divine judgment against America, it was a terrible display of violence. In its aftermath Americans packed churches and cried out to God. While people all too quickly went back to sleep, there was at least a brief, intense time of awareness and awakening.

The result of God's judgment in Ezekiel 38–39 will be similar, yet real and lasting. Still, even people from those nations that have come against God and Israel will have an opportunity to acknowledge the greatness and grace of God and be delivered from their sins. Old Testament scholar Christopher J. H. Wright reminds us, "As God's redeemed people we cannot contemplate the ultimate defeat of evil and the destruction of the wicked with any sense of moral superiority. For we know that apart from the grace of God which has brought us to repentance and restoration, the same fate would justly await us."[17]

CONCLUSIONS

There are numerous conclusions to draw from Ezekiel 38–39, but here are a few for you to gather your thoughts around.

- An axis of nations that surround Israel—the far enemies or outer ring of nations—will conspire and come against Israel in the latter years to get rid of Israel once and for all. We see this alliance merging today.
- The invasion of Israel will be a surprise attack, occurring during the first half of the seven-year Tribulation, when Israel is living in peace and prosperity under a coming peace treaty that will be forged by the Antichrist. The number one issue in the Middle East today is the yearning for peace between Israel, the Palestinians, and Israel's other near neighbors.
- Satan is the invisible spiritual force behind the obsession in Iran to wipe Israel off the map.

- When Israel is invaded and it appears that she is finished, God will dramatically intervene to destroy the avalanche of allies and will even send shock waves of judgment against the homeland of the invaders.
- God's demonstration of power and greatness will be so overwhelming that the nations will be forced to acknowledge that He alone is the true God.
- The people of Israel will begin to recognize there is no one like their God and will experience a turning to the Lord.
- God is sovereign. He controls nations and nature. No one can stand against Him.
- God is the only Savior. He is the only One who can deliver nations and individuals.
- Salvation is found in no one else. Turning to Him and trusting in Him is your only hope. Jesus is coming for those who have come to Him.

CHAPTER 7

APPROACHING MIDNIGHT

IN THE U.S. CAPITOL, at the entrance to the Statuary Hall (the original chamber for the House of Representatives), you can find one of the oldest works of art in the building. It's a massive timepiece called the Car of History. Positioned above this clock is Clio, the muse of history. In her hand is a book, in which she records the events of history as they unfold.

In 1999, in a speech before a joint session of Congress, historian and Pulitzer Prize winner David McCullough said of this clock: "It is also a clock with two hands and an old-fashioned face. The kind that shows what time it is now . . . what time it used to be . . . what time it will become."

God also has a clock that tells what time it is now and what time it will become. His divine timepiece is the nation and people of Israel. The late pastor Adrian Rogers summed up Israel's place in God's prophetic program:

> These are dangerous days in which we live! The storm clouds are gathering. The lightning is flashing—and the

> lightning rod is Israel. Christians cannot deny or ignore the significance of the nation of Israel . . . The eyes of the entire world are upon the tiny state of Israel, and your eyes need to be there too, because the Jews and Israel are the people and the land of destiny. As the Jew goes, so goes the world. Israel is God's yardstick. Israel is God's measuring rod. Israel is God's blueprint. Israel is God's program for what He is doing in the world.[1]

Charles H. Dyer, an expert in Middle Eastern history and geography, wrote, "God gave Israel a starring role in His drama of the ages, and Israel will again take center stage in the final act. You cannot understand the future without understanding the part assigned to Israel."[2] Israel is mentioned more than twenty-five hundred times in the Bible. After almost two thousand years of dispersion to more than seventy countries, the modern state of Israel was founded and formed in 1948. The Jewish people are still in the process of being regathered to their ancient homeland.

Their regathering to their land has set off a firestorm in the Middle East. Israel is surrounded by enemies who want her driven into the sea. The animosity of the nations against Israel that will prevail in the end times was prophesied by Zechariah about five hundred years before the coming of Christ.

> The burden of the word of the Lord concerning Israel. Thus declares the Lord who stretches out the heavens, lays the foundation of the earth, and forms the

> spirit of man within him, "Behold, I am going to make Jerusalem a cup that causes reeling to all the peoples around; and when the siege is against Jerusalem, it will also be against Judah. It will come about in that day that I will make Jerusalem a heavy stone for all the peoples; all who lift it will be severely injured. And all the nations of the earth will be gathered against it." (Zechariah 12:1–3)

What's happening in Israel today bears a remarkable correspondence to this ancient prophecy but even more specifically to the war in Ezekiel 38–39. Israel is at war. She has been at war with Iran since the Islamic Revolution in 1979.

Iran's mullah regime detests Israel. So do Iran's elite military units. This was evidenced at a graduation ceremony of Iranian officers of the Revolutionary Guard Academy. During the ceremony Iranian officers had an Israeli flag painted on the bottom of their boots that could be seen clearly as they goose-stepped like Nazi troops of the 1930s. Iran wants to put its boot on Israel's neck. The obsession of every Iranian soldier is the subjugation of Israel under the heel of Iranian power. Speaking of Israel, a top Iranian general in charge of Iran's Revolutionary Guards said, "This sinister regime must be wiped off the map and this is no longer a dream but it is an achievable goal."[3]

Iran's premier clandestine military unit, which functions under Iran's Revolutionary Guard is called the Quds

Force. The Arabic name for Jerusalem is Al Quds. This name was selected to be a constant reminder of Iran's relentless desire to recapture Jerusalem and put it under Shiite control. All of this fits the prophecy of Ezekiel 38 to a tee.

THE REAL SHADOW WAR

Iranian efforts to annihilate Israel are occurring against the dark backdrop of increasing global antisemitism. Hatred for Israel today is present in its most concentrated form in Iran, but antisemitism is increasing at an alarming rate worldwide. We all see it. Synagogues are regularly the scenes of ruthless slaughter. It's open season on the Jewish people. The resurgence of rage against Israel is palpable. Here are just a few of the acts of antisemitism that made news throughout 2025:

- *January 21:* A childcare center in Sydney was set alight and antisemitic graffiti was sprayed on the wall.
- *February 21:* An attacker stabbed a man at Berlin's Holocaust memorial.
- *May 22:* Two Israeli embassy staffers were killed by a lone gunman in Washington, DC.
- *August 31:* A Holocaust memorial in the French city of Lyon was defaced, with the words "Free Gaza" etched into a black marble stele.

- *September 8:* Two Palestinian gunmen opened fire at a bus stop on the outskirts of Jerusalem, killing six people.
- *October 2:* A man drove a car into pedestrians and stabbed a security guard, killing at least two people and seriously injuring three more at a synagogue in Manchester where worshippers were marking Yom Kippur.[4]

This trend had already been growing before 2025. In 2023, for example, the Anti-Defamation League, a Jewish advocacy group, recorded 8,873 antisemitic incidents in the U.S., a 140 percent increase over the previous year, "and a record high since it began keeping track in 1979."[5]

Sadly, this is nothing new. Antisemitism is as old as Abraham. Through the millennia, there have been numerous attempts to wipe out the Jews. The Jewish people have been the victims of age-long persecution and pogroms to exterminate their race. But the recent increase in antisemitism is striking.

Have you ever wondered why there is so much pent-up hatred for the Jewish people and the state of Israel? Why won't it go away? Why has it persisted for so long? While persecutors of the Jewish people down through the ages have had their own evil justifications for their actions, there are two main underlying reasons behind the hatred of Israel and desire to drive them out of their land.

First, and more specifically, the clash between the Jewish people and their neighbors goes back four thousand years to the days of Abraham and his two sons. The central issue is: Who owns the land? According to Genesis 12:1–3 and 15:15–21, God made an eternal covenant with Abraham giving him the promised land. The borders of the land are carefully outlined in Genesis 15:18–21. The covenant blessings and land promise were transferred to Abraham's son Isaac, not Ishmael. Centuries later, when Islam came along, the story was changed to highlight Ishmael in place of Isaac.

Muslims believe Abraham took Ishmael to Mount Moriah instead of Isaac (Genesis 22). They maintain that Abraham and Hagar fled to Mecca with Ishmael where he became a prophet and an ancestor to Muhammad. The Bible is clear that God blessed Ishmael. "As for Ishmael, I have heard you; behold, I will bless him, and will make him fruitful and will multiply him exceedingly. He shall become the father of twelve princes, and I will make him a great nation" (Genesis 17:20).

Nevertheless, the promised land was deeded by God forever to Abraham and then to Isaac and then to Isaac's son Jacob and his descendants. The Jewish people own the land, the city of Jerusalem, and the Temple Mount, according to the Bible. Yet, Muslims believe it belongs to them. Therein lies the historical rivalry and hostility.

Iranians are not descendants of Ishmael; they are Persians. Some Arabs today are not descendants of Ishmael, but many are. Regardless, followers of Islam believe the land is theirs by divine right. The battle for the land of Israel we see today stems from this ancient rivalry four millennia in the making.

Second, the primary driving force behind antisemitism in general is the devil, God's enemy, Satan. Satan is anti-Christ and antisemitic. Satan hates what God loves, so he hates Jesus, and he hates the Jewish people because God has a purpose and plan for the Jewish people in the end of days. God promised the Jewish people a specific piece of real estate in the Middle East in Genesis 15:18–21, and He gave it to them as their possession forever. Jesus is coming back someday to fulfill that promise to Israel. He will bring the Jewish people into their promised land under His rule.

God also promised that a Messiah from the line of King David would rule over Israel in their land. To prevent the fulfillment of that prophecy, Satan worked throughout the Old Testament to wipe out the Jewish people and specifically the line of David to keep Jesus from being born. When that failed, he tempted Jesus to sin, to disqualify Him from being the Savior (Matthew 4). When he was unsuccessful in that ploy, Satan moved the Jewish leaders and the Romans to kill Him. But Jesus came back to life on the third day (Matthew 27–28).

Satan's last-ditch effort to derail God's program and defeat God's promises to Abraham and David is to eliminate the Jewish people. In so doing, Satan can thwart the promises of God. He can prevent Jesus from ruling over the Jewish people as promised. This explains the irrational hatred Israel's neighbors have for the Jewish state and the Jewish people. They are driven by a demonically inspired detestation of Israel.

Make no mistake. Satan is the world's greatest anti-Semite. That explains the dark agenda against Israel and the gathering storm in the Middle East. It explains why events are building in the Middle East to a grand climax. And it explains Iran's obsession with eliminating Israel from the map and its continuing plan, despite recent setbacks, to rejuvenate its surrogates and encircle Israel in a ring of fire.

CONCLUSION

Ironically, the Iranian regime in Tehran that is energized by a Satanic hatred for Israel is fixated on destroying the "Great Satan" (America) and the "Little Satan" (Israel). As we've seen, recent military setbacks have left Iran more desperate than ever: Assad's regime has fallen in Syria, Hezbollah has been significantly degraded in Lebanon, and Israel has struck Iran's nuclear facilities. A cornered regime with limited options may be more likely to risk everything in the desperate gambit described in Ezekiel 38–39. This ancient prophecy, written around 571 B.C., prophesies an invasion of Israel by a coalition of Islamic nations, including Iran as a key player.

The war of Gog and Magog hasn't occurred yet, but the great storm prophesied in Ezekiel is coming. How soon it will happen is outside our current ability to know. However, Israel's war with Iran and its proxies is a major piece to the puzzle that seems to be falling into place.

Keep watching the Middle East. But remember: Israel is God's prophetic clock—and the hands are approaching midnight.

ISRAEL'S FUTURE IN SEVEN WORDS

- **TREATY**: Under the direction of a Western leader, the Antichrist, who will guarantee peace and security, Israel will ink a treaty with him and possibly her neighbors (Daniel 9:27).
- **TEMPLE**: Israel will build the third temple in the end times (Matthew 24:15; 2 Thessalonians 2:4; Revelation 11:1–2).
- **TRAP**: The Battle of Gog and Magog will be a surprise attack when Israel has let down her guard under the treaty with the West (Ezekiel 38–39).
- **TRAITOR**: With the power vacuum created by the destruction of the Russian-Islamic axis, the Antichrist will break his treaty with Israel at the midpoint and consolidate his global rule (Daniel 9:27).
- **TROUBLE**: Israel will endure the great Tribulation (Jeremiah 30:7).
- **TURNING**: As Christ returns to earth, many in Israel will turn to Him and receive Him as Messiah and Lord (Zechariah 12:10).

- **TRIUMPH:** Jesus will come to rescue the remnant of Israel and establish His one-thousand-year reign on the earth. During this era, the covenants God made with Israel will be literally and completely fulfilled (Revelation 20:1–6).

CHAPTER 8

WILL AMERICA SURVIVE?

America is in trouble. Big trouble. As a nation we are dancing on a perilous precipice, teetering on the verge of destruction. Aside from known threats of global terror, a Middle East meltdown, a soaring national debt, and the divisive spirit that has split our nation in two, our country's very foundations are cracking beneath our feet. America is losing her *soul.*

—*Jeff Kinley, The End of America*

IT IS SAID that in the year 1787, a Scottish history professor named Alexander Fraser Tytler observed the following about the longevity of democracy:

> A democracy is always temporary in nature; it simply cannot exist as a permanent form of government. A democracy will continue to exist up until the time that voters discover that they can vote themselves generous gifts from the public treasury. From that

> moment on, the majority always votes for the candidates who promise the most benefits from the public treasury, with the result that every democracy will finally collapse due to loose fiscal policy, which is always followed by a dictatorship.
>
> The average age of the world's greatest civilizations from the beginning of history has been about two hundred years. During those two hundred years, these nations always progressed through the following sequence:
>
> From bondage to spiritual faith;
> From spiritual faith to great courage;
> From courage to liberty;
> From liberty to abundance;
> From abundance to complacency;
> From complacency to apathy;
> From apathy to dependence;
> From dependence back into bondage.[1]

Based on any realistic evaluation, America is sliding toward the bottom of Professor Tytler's list. Abundance, apathy, and complacency abound. Dependence and bondage could be waiting in the wings.

The United States, while still prospering financially and wielding great military might, seems to be in trouble on numerous fronts. The status of the world's greatest superpower is not as firm as it has been in the past. Current events are magnifying cracks in the foundation.

From the prophetic perspective, this raises important questions—questions about what role, if any, America plays in the end-time picture set forth in the Bible. When considering the showdown with Iran, and all its prophetic implications for Israel, the world, and the Middle East, it's fitting to briefly assess America's future. The place of America in Bible prophecy is probably the most asked question about the end times.

AMERICAN ABSENCE

An impressive list of modern nations (or their ancient counterpart) are referenced in end-time prophecies found in Scripture.

Israel
Jordan (Ammon, Moab, and Edom)
Egypt
Sudan (Cush)
Russia (Rosh)
Iran (Persia)
Iraq (Babylon)
Europe (reunited Roman Empire)
Central Asia (Magog)
Syria
Greece

Saudi Arabia and other Gulf States (Sheba and Dedan)
Libya (Put)
Lebanon (Tyre)

Some would add China or other Far Eastern nations to this list. They find them in the reference to the "kings from the east" in Revelation 16:12.

Noticeably absent from this list is America. All agree that America is never explicitly mentioned in the pages of Scripture. The Bible never uses the word "America," nor does it say, "the United States." However, through the years, prophecy teachers have isolated several scriptures they believe could be symbolic references to America. Some of the more notable ones are:

- The unnamed nation in Isaiah 18
- The "young lions" or "merchants of Tarshish" in Ezekiel 38:13
- Babylon the Great in Revelation 17–18

There's another view that holds America is the ten lost tribes of Israel.

Having examined each of these views in detail, I don't believe any of them directly refer to America.[2] I don't believe America is mentioned *directly* or *indirectly* in Scripture. Joel Rosenberg agrees:

> The truth is, the United States of America simply is nowhere to be found in the Bible. This may be painful for many to hear. This may be difficult for many to accept. Nevertheless, the fact remains: The US is never directly mentioned or specifically referenced in Bible history or in Bible prophecy. It just isn't.[3]

America's absence from the end-time picture raises the "why" question. Why is America missing in action in end-time prophecy? One obvious possibility is that America is simply not mentioned, just like most other nations. End-time prophecy shines the spotlight primarily on Israel and the Middle East, so America may just be omitted for that reason. While that's certainly possible, end-time prophecies do include Russia, Turkey, and the kings of the East, all of which lie outside the Middle East, so including America would not necessarily be a stretch. So what are we to make, if anything, of the scriptural silence concerning America in the end times?

While there is certainly room for disagreement on this point, I believe the lack of any mention of America in the end times is a clue that something must happen to America to lower her from superpower status before the end times begin. After all, it would be strange to omit any reference to the world's greatest superpower in end-time events if America is still the greatest nation on earth. Assuming it's true that America's absence from end-time prophecy is an indication that America is no longer the world's dominant power, what will happen to significantly decrease America's influence? What are some plausible scenarios to explain American absence from end-time prophecy?

Let me briefly suggest five possibilities.

1. ECONOMIC IMPLOSION

While considering possible reasons for the future fall of the United States, the list must include the growing debt bomb. The US total debt and annual budget deficit continue to balloon with no end in sight. The numbers have grown so large that it's difficult to wrap our minds around. America is now closing in on $40 trillion in debt and counting . . . and counting. The US treasury racks up an additional trillion every 365 days. The national debt is a whopping 125 percent GDP. America is drowning in debt—swamped to spending, and even more troubling is that few seem to be worried about it. Politicians, for the most part, go on as if a day of reckoning will never come.

One problem we all face is that the human mind has trouble understanding a figure so massive. Here are some shocking facts that help put into perspective just how large $23 trillion really is.

- To pay down our national debt you would have to combine the GDP of China, Japan, and India.
- The United States owes $110,000 *per citizen.*

- The United States owes $286,000 *per taxpayer.*
- The United States currently has $73–175 trillion in unfunded liabilities.
- Interest on the national debt exceeds annual spending on Medicare, as well as national defense.[4]
- Modern presidents have doubled the national debt every nine years.[5]

To balance this gloomy debt picture, it's important to note that the US economy has enjoyed a great run over the past few years. The fiscal policies of President Trump have created increased wealth and prosperity in every stratum of society. Unemployment is down, earnings are up, and the stock market has performed well. The bulls are running. But how much longer can the reckless spending spree go on? When will the debt anchor exert such a downward pull that meaningful recovery is no longer feasible? When will America run out of money to fund her military and defend herself?

Runaway debt, ending in economic implosion, could spell American decline and even disaster

2. NUCLEAR NIGHTMARE

Another circumstance that could bring about America's demise is a nuclear 9/11. As nuclear proliferation spirals out of control, rogue nations such as Pakistan, North Korea, or Iran—if and when they get the bomb—could transfer a nuclear device or even a dirty bomb to a terrorist cell to detonate on American soil. Nuclear terror could trigger all kinds of consequences, bringing America to its knees.

3. MORAL CAVE-IN

God is merciful and patient. We should all be thankful for His goodness and grace to sinners, demonstrated in the sacrifice of Jesus. Nevertheless, the Bible is clear that God's wrath is not stored up forever. The righteous, holy God is justly angry against human sin. His judgment falls on nations as well as individuals.

The wrath of God is not an immensely popular topic today. It has never been popular. However, the Bible presents at least four aspects of God's wrath.

1. **DIRECT WRATH** is a cataclysmic outpouring of God's judgment. Some examples of this are the global flood (Genesis 7–8), the destruction of Sodom and Gomorrah (Genesis 19), and the plagues of Egypt (Exodus 7–11).
2. **ESCHATOLOGICAL OR END-TIME WRATH** (also known as "Day of the Lord wrath") is the judgment of God poured out on earth during the future time of global Tribulation described in Revelation 6–19. The New Testament teaches that the church of Jesus Christ will be exempted from this time of wrath

(1 Thessalonians 1:9–10; 5:9; Revelation 3:10–11). Jesus will come to rescue His bride before it begins.

3. **ETERNAL WRATH** is the final form of God's wrath in the lake of fire, where the lost will experience separation from God (Revelation 14:9–11; 20:10, 15).
4. **ABANDONMENT WRATH** is a lesser-known form of God's wrath. It occurs when God actively pushes a person or nation in the direction they've already chosen and then removes His hand, "letting go" of that person or nation without any blessing or intervention to help them.

So far, by God's grace, America has not experienced the direct wrath of God, but could the United States be suffering abandonment wrath that will lead to an outpouring of God's direct wrath? Are there signs it has begun? How can we know? What does that look like?

Romans 1:21–32 is the clearest passage in the New Testament on God's "letting go" of a person or nation. Notice the threefold repetition of the words "God gave them over" (Romans 1:24, 26, 28). This is the wrath of abandonment—God removing His hand and His help. These verses reveal that abandonment wrath unfolds little by little. It's a deadly, downward spiral. "Abandonment is a gradual release that occurs in stages. And yet, like birth pangs, it seems to intensify toward a dramatic climax of corruption."[6] Four stages or phases can be traced in Romans 1:21–32.

- **STAGE 1—REJECTION OF GOD:** "For even though they knew God, they did not honor Him as God or give thanks, but they became futile in their speculations, and their foolish heart was darkened. Professing to be wise, they became fools, and exchanged the glory of the incorruptible God for an image in the form of corruptible man and of birds and four-footed animals and crawling creatures." (Romans 1:21–23)
- **STAGE 2—RAMPANT SEXUAL IMMORALITY:** "Therefore God gave them over in the lusts of their hearts to impurity, so that their bodies would be dishonored among them. For they exchanged the truth of God for a lie, and worshiped and served the creature rather than the Creator, who is blessed forever. Amen." (Romans 1:24–25)
- **STAGE 3—REVOLUTION OF HOMOSEXUALITY:** "For this reason God gave them over to degrading passions; for their women exchanged the natural function for that which is unnatural, and in the same way also the men abandoned the natural function of the woman and burned in their desire toward one another, men with men committing indecent acts and receiving in their own persons the due penalty of their error." (Roman 1:26–27)
- **STAGE 4—RATIFICATION OF EVIL:** "And just as they did not see fit to acknowledge God any longer, God gave them over to a depraved mind, to do those things which are not proper, being filled with

> all unrighteousness, wickedness, greed, evil; full of envy, murder, strife, deceit, malice; they are gossips, slanderers, haters of God, insolent, arrogant, boastful, inventors of evil, disobedient to parents, without understanding, untrustworthy, unloving, unmerciful; and although they know the ordinance of God, that those who practice such things are worthy of death, they not only do the same, but also give hearty approval to those who practice them." (Romans 1:28–32)

The presence and progression of these stages does not indicate that God will judge a nation but that He already is judging. According to Romans 1, America is already under the judgment of God.

Rejection of God is the first domino that triggers the moral meltdown. That's stage 1 in the abandonment cycle—rejecting God. Tragically, when people lose God, they lose themselves, and moral confusion and chaos ensue. By any metric, we've witnessed a seismic moral shift in America in the past two decades. Moral thresholds are being crossed with alarming speed. Just when you think it can't get any worse, another descending step is uncovered. We live in a *Fifty Shades of Grey* culture. Pornography is pervasive. Here are just a few sobering statistics.

- There are twenty-five million pornographic websites.
- Forty million people regularly visit these sites.

- Almost eight in ten Americans visit a pornographic website at least once a month.[7]

American society is soaked in sexual sin. That's stage 2.

The atrocity of abortion stalks our land. Thankfully, abortion rates in America are steadily declining, but the tragic news is that the number is still close to one million per year!

One of the signs that a nation is being abandoned by God is the acceptance and sanctioning of homosexuality. Today in America, same-sex marriage is settled law. Any opposition to same-sex marriage or even questioning of it brings the wrath of the culture and the media. Gender confusion is growing. Transgenderism and "gender fluidity" are proliferating. Gender options today range anywhere from two to eighty-two. That's stage 3.

As Main Thing Ministries founder Jeff Kinley noted, "Spiritual decadence is a black hole, and its gravitational pull is sucking our nation into inescapable darkness."[8] Immorality of every kind is not just tolerated, it's protected and celebrated. That's stage 4.

America appears to be on the road to divine abandonment. This could be another leading factor in America's final fall.

4. CIVIL WAR II

One frightening possibility that could explain America's absence from end-time prophecy and apparent demise is a civil war—a total fracturing and dissolution of the nation. This would have been unthinkable even a few years ago, but the chasm between left and right is widening to what increasingly looks like a point of no return. Rabid partisanship and poisonous politics are rampant on every conceivable issue. The middle of the road seems to be the road less traveled than ever before.

In light of the rising polarization in our public discourse in recent years, talk of a second US civil war has increased. When I first heard about this, I thought it was nothing more than further reckless rhetoric by conspiracy theorists and fanatics, which I try to avoid. However, a growing number of respected experts are noting that the political environment in the United States is the most divided it's been since the Civil War. Political analyst Bill Schneider, a professor of policy, government, and international affairs at George Mason University, opines, "Nothing is ever permanent, but we are broken. I'd say this is the most divided we've been since the Civil War."[9]

There's no doubt the United States is currently locked in a fierce ideological, political, and cultural civil war. Few would dispute that. Some refer to the current state of affairs as a "soft" civil war that's already underway in America, observed in the tearing of the racial, political, social, and ideological fabric. But could the ideological, political civil war spiral out of control, overflow the banks, and descend into a violent war? More and more people seem to think so.

Steve Chapman, a member of the *Chicago Tribune*'s editorial board, observed:

> Modern America is sharply polarized, battered by political furies and divided as never before. Moderation is disappearing, we are told, as Americans increasingly shun people of different views. We are split between hostile groups, each with its own TV networks, fast-food chains and sporting apparel—Fox News vs. MSNBC, Chick-fil-A vs. Chipotle, Under Armour vs. Nike. . . . Extreme, vocal ideologues are gaining ground on both the right and the left. One-third of likely voters, a poll found, think we are on the verge of civil war.[10]

Speaking after the House voted along party lines to approve a measure establishing procedures for the impeachment inquiry, Representative Louie Gohmert, a Republican from Texas, said that House Democrats were "about to push this country to a civil war if they were to get their wishes." He then added, "And if there's one thing I don't want to see in my lifetime, I don't want to ever have participation in, it's a civil war. Some historian, I don't remember who, said, guns are only involved in the last phase of a civil war."[11]

Civil war is a scary scenario to even think about, but more and more the ingredients seem to be simmering. Polarization abounds on every front. The nation is divided into two hostile camps on almost every issue. Common ground and compromise are increasingly elusive. President Trump has become a lightning rod for the Left. Commentator and political analyst Bill O'Reilly notes:

> As a person who loves America and many of the people in it, the specter of a civil war over Donald Trump is depressing. But that's exactly what's happening. . . . As things continue to devolve, anger is growing on both sides but more in the pro-Trump precincts. I fear violence might be next.[12]

Ray Dalio, who has accurately predicted many major downturns in the US in recent decades, addressed the issue of an impending civil war in an interview with Fortune magazine, which summarized his warning:

> Rising US debt and deepening political divisions could push the country toward crisis. . . . America faces a choice between uniting around shared interests or descending into destructive conflict. . . . The nation's 125 percent debt-to-GDP ratio risks triggering a "debt bomb" if investors lose confidence, forcing higher borrowing costs or painful spending cuts. Should friction in the US continue, . . . individuals' ability to "hurt each other" has never been higher.

The *Fortune* article went on to quote these words from Dalio: "We're in wars. There is a financial, money war. There's a technology war, there's geopolitical wars, and there are more military wars. And so we have a civil war of some sort which is developing in the US and elsewhere, where there are irreconcilable differences."[13]

A recent Gallup survey found 80 percent of Americans

believed their country was "greatly divided" on key issues.[14]

Many triggers for a second civil war are possible. The following list is a rundown of some of the more conspicuous recent flashpoints.

- anarchist groups such as Antifa
- racial tensions
- white supremacists
- angry clashes over the meaning and extent of the Second Amendment
- constant partisan committee hearings in Congress
- immigration and ICE deportations
- global warming
- capitalism versus socialism / communism
- talk of certain states seceding from the Union
- Senate hearings for Supreme Court nominations
- constant threats of presidential impeachment
- Donald Trump, the president of the United States, being unwelcome and even actively excluded from many cities in America
- celebrities being blacklisted for showing friendliness to the president

A *Washington Post* headline reads, "In America, talk turns to something not spoken of for 150 years: Civil war." The story references, among others, Stanford University historian Victor Davis Hanson, who asked in a *National Review* essay last summer, "How, when, and why has the United States now arrived at the brink of a veritable civil war?" Dr. Hanson warns, "Almost every cultural and social institution—universities, the public schools, the NFL, the Oscars, the Tonys, the Grammys, late-night television, public restaurants, coffee shops, movies, TV, stand-up comedy—has been not just politicized but also weaponized. [The US stands] at the brink of a veritable civil war."[15]

The idea of civil war may not be as far-fetched as some believe. "The saber-rattling is getting louder. Governors. Judges. Preachers. Politicians. [As well as Podcasters.] All are ramping up the rhetoric, pushing the deep political divide within the United States towards a second Civil War."[16]

We pray this will never happen, but it could, and it would plunge the United States into oblivion.

5. THE GREAT DISAPPEARANCE

While any of these scenarios are possible alone or in a deadly combination, taking all the facts into account, my view is that the final fall of America will occur as a result of the rapture of all believers to heaven. The Bible predicts that a day is coming when the bride of Jesus Christ will be suddenly whisked away to heaven in the time it takes to blink. All over the earth, believers will suddenly disappear.

The rapture is not an event that was made up by wishful believers. Belief in the rapture is based on the clear teaching of Scripture. In John 14:1–3, Jesus promised to come back for His followers to take them to heaven.

> "Do not let your heart be troubled; believe in God, believe also in Me. In My Father's house are many dwelling places; if it were not so, I would have told you; for I go to prepare a place for you. If I go and prepare a place for you, I will come again and receive you to Myself, that where I am, there you may be also."

The apostle Paul spoke often of the coming of Christ to remove or rapture His people from earth to heaven.

> Behold, I tell you a mystery; we will not all sleep, but we will all be changed, in a moment, in the twinkling of an eye, at the last trumpet; for the trumpet will sound, and the dead will be raised imperishable, and we will be changed. For the perishable must put on the imperishable, and this mortal must put on immortality. (1 Corinthians 15:51–53)

Writing to the Thessalonians, Paul highlighted the resurrection of deceased believers and the rapture of those who are alive when Jesus comes.

> For this we say to you by the word of the Lord, that we who are alive and remain until the coming of the Lord, will not precede those who have fallen asleep.

> For the Lord Himself will descend from heaven with a shout, with the voice of the archangel and with the trumpet of God, and the dead in Christ will rise first. Then we who are alive and remain will be caught up together with them in the clouds to meet the Lord in the air, and so we shall always be with the Lord. Therefore comfort one another with these words. (1 Thessalonians 4:15–18)

The words "caught up" in 1 Thessalonians 4:17 translate the Greek word *harpazo*, which refers to the catching away of the church to heaven. When the Bible was translated from Greek to Latin by Jerome, he translated the word *harpazo* with the Latin word *rapio*, from which we get our English word *rapture*. The concept of a future rapture, or catching away of believers to heaven, is based on sound scriptural interpretation.

When the rapture occurs, every believer in America and all over the earth will be immediately transported to heaven, leaving those who are left behind to pick up the pieces of a shriveled workforce and shattered economy, not to mention the psychological trauma and fear that will prevail. While there are believers in every nation, about 5 to 10 percent of Americans profess faith in Jesus Christ alone for salvation from sin. The sudden removal of twenty to thirty million people from the United States would be apocalyptic (literally).

Prophecy teacher Jeff Kinley painted a graphic picture of America in the aftermath of the rapture:

> So imagine what will happen when both the salt and the light is removed from today's culture. Who will be left behind to preserve decency, morality, and goodness? Who will expose and penetrate the darkness? . . . Not a single believer on American soil. Imagine that for a moment. . . . With our country's soul now removed, she will become a zombie-like nation, wandering aimlessly toward her ultimate and inevitable demise. . . . In this miraculous moment, the complete departure of Christians is not the only thing that will change. Everything will be altered following that split-second departure—governments, states, communities, militaries, schools, churches, hospitals, universities, families, marriages, national infrastructures . . . *everything*. There won't be a single pocket of society that remains unaffected, as for all practical purposes, God will have "left the building."[17]

Kinley concluded his somber description of post-rapture America:

> What follows is political, economic, and moral chaos in this country. . . . A colossal void of truth will be left behind. And unrestrained sin will begin swallowing up an entire society. All across the country, the scenario will become one of confusion, chaos, and fear, resulting in rampant crime, robberies, and murders. A nationwide panic attack will grip the country. . . . Because of the rapture, a sizable portion of America's

> population will be gone, leaving huge voids in virtually every strata [*sic*] of society. . . . With anarchy and chaos reigning, America will be paralyzed, and officially no longer a major player in world affairs.
>
> Like a heavy blanket, darkness falls on an entire nation. . . . In the time it takes you to bat an eye, our country will be transformed from the Land of the Free to the Home of the Abandoned. Before the sun rises, she will go from being a global superpower to a drowning nation struggling to survive. . . . It's Jesus's rescue of His bride from a rebellious planet that will pull the pin, ignite public pandemonium, and usher in an unprecedented moment in human history.[18]

Of course, the rapture could occur in concert with some of the other scenarios outlined above, plunging the late great United States into a national free fall.

KEEP GOING

While no one on earth knows for sure what will happen to the United States in the end times, the lack of any biblical mention of America as a key player does not bode well for continued American greatness and dominance.

Knowing this should not cause us to give up and do nothing—to throw up our hands in despair. We need to continue to do three main things. First, fervently pray for our nation and its leaders every day (1 Timothy 2:1–2).

Second, we must strive to live godly, righteous lives as salt and light in an increasingly decaying and darkening world. Proverbs 14:34 reminds us that "righteousness exalts a nation."

Third, America needs to maintain support for Israel, so she can experience the promise to those who bless Israel (Genesis 12:1–3). I don't mean we have to support every decision Israel makes. It's a nation ruled by fallen human beings just like the rest of us. What I mean is that we must support Israel's right to their ancient homeland. President Trump has honored the Jewish people by recognizing the Golan Heights as part of Israeli territory, declaring that Israeli settlements in the West Bank do not violate international law, and bringing an end to the Israel-Gaza War. In spite of the United States' shortcomings, I believe God's hand of blessing remains upon this land, at least to some degree, for our support of Israel.

We do all these things as we await the coming of Jesus. No one knows when He will come. We need to be ready all the time and do what we can while we can in His service.

CHAPTER 9

LIVING LIKE THERE'S NO TOMORROW

WHEN I WAS GROWING UP, I had a friend down the street whose mother loved puzzles. Really big, complicated puzzles with very small pieces. I was never patient enough to put together any puzzle that took longer than an hour, so I was amazed by these puzzles that would fill an entire table in their game room for months at a time as she carefully plugged each piece in place. Watching the process, I learned that a puzzle master must consult the picture on the top of the box as the template for the final product. You have to have the final picture in view. I also learned that the best way to construct a puzzle is to begin with the corner and edge pieces to establish a frame and then to work toward the middle.

The same is true of the end-time prophetic puzzle. The end-time picture set forth in Scripture is the picture on top of the box. When all the pieces are finally in place, that's what it will look like. As we look at our world today, events are beginning to closely match the picture on the puzzle box. All the puzzle pieces aren't in place, but the corners and edges have taken form. The framework is set. The center of the puzzle is ready to be filled in.

Israel is back in her ancient homeland after almost two thousand years of dispersion. Antisemitism is surging. Russia is rising. Iran is increasing. Russia, Iran, and Turkey are allied for the first time in history. The alliance of Ezekiel 38 is developing and deepening. Iran, Israel, and the United States have moved past the brink of war—a cold war—to hot war. Current events resemble the prophetic puzzle in Ezekiel 38—39 more and more as each day passes.

This raises a critical question: How should we live in light of what's unfolding in our world? In light of what lies ahead? What should we do? How can we find peace as the storm clouds gather and make sure we're ready when Jesus comes? Many people have the mistaken idea that Bible prophecy isn't relevant to everyday life. That it has no practical application. I disagree. Bible prophecy is supremely relevant and practical. God gave prophecy to change our hearts, not to cram our heads with knowledge. Eschatology leads to ethics. Believing Jesus can come at any moment must change what we do and what we don't do.

While there are many practical implications of knowing what's coming, let me suggest five simple, practical points of application for you to make part of your thinking and living that will make a difference in your life today.

1. RECOGNIZE THE BIBLE IS TRUE

Humans can't resist the temptation to try to forecast the future. This inclination increases in troubled times. But man's résumé of accurately predicting the future is very thin. We don't even know what will happen tomorrow. But the Bible does. There's an old saying, "If you want to know what happened yesterday, read the newspaper; if you want to know what happened today, listen to the evening news; if you want to know what will happen tomorrow, read the Bible." As we've seen, the Bible is a book of prophecy. Hundreds of prophecies have been fulfilled, many related to ancient Persia—modern-day Iran.

While the rise of militant Islam has shocked and surprised most people, amazingly, more than twenty-five hundred years ago, God, through the prophet Ezekiel, predicted the exact scenario that we see developing before our eyes every day on the evening news. Ezekiel 36–39 is "history written beforehand." It foretells the regathering of the Jewish people to their ancient homeland, the animosity the surrounding nations will have for Israel, and the invasion of Israel by those nations.

God predicted all these things with piercing precision.

Seven times in Ezekiel 38–39 we read the same words, "Thus says the Lord God" (38:3, 10, 14, 17; 39:1, 17, 25). Another eight times we see the refrain, "declares the Lord God." Obviously, God doesn't want us to miss the point—this is His Word. The prediction in Ezekiel 38–39 comes directly from Him. He is the author of the script. The Bible is true. Fulfilled prophecy proves it.

We can rest assured that the biblical predictions that are still unfulfilled will happen. We can also rest assured that what the Bible tells us about God, Jesus, salvation, sin, and our own lives is trustworthy and reliable.

So, recognize the Bible is true and to read it regularly. Soak in its truth and apply its instruction to your daily life. It will transform you.

2. REALIZE YOUR NEED FOR JESUS

The Bible not only accurately predicts the future, it also accurately portrays the human condition apart from God. The inspired, inerrant Word of God truthfully, transparently diagnoses the condition of every person. It tells that we have all sinned and are falling short of God's righteous standard (Romans 3:23). That's the bad news—the *really* bad news. Every person on earth is sinful and separated from God. We constantly miss the mark of perfection. We're born that way. And there's nothing on our own we can do about our predicament. No amount of church attendance, good works, helping the poor, or praying can ever forgive our sins.

You and I can't get rid of one of our sins on our own, let alone the thousands of transgressions that pile up throughout our lives. The Bible is clear that our sins can only be washed away by the blood of Jesus Christ, that is, His death for us. His death in our place.

Jesus is the only Mediator, the only go-between who can bridge the chasm between a holy God and sinful people. He is your only hope for heaven. No one will be in heaven without personally trusting in Him for salvation.

If you've never received Jesus as your Savior from sin, that's the first thing you need to do before you do anything else. He is life. He is truth. He is the way to God. Here are three simple steps to guide you to trusting in Jesus.

First, *admit* you're a sinner. That shouldn't be too difficult to do. We all know the guilt we feel when we do things that hurt others or ourselves. You and I know we're sinful and fallen.

Second, *acknowledge* that you can't do anything to save yourself—that you need a Savior.

Third, *accept* Jesus Christ as your Savior. He's the Savior you need. Receive the payment He offered on the cross for your sins. The Bible says we become children of God, part of His family, by receiving Jesus as our Savior and Lord (John 1:12–13).

Why not receive Him now? Why not receive the pardon He purchased for you when He died on the cross and rose again on the third day?

3. REMEMBER GOD IS IN CONTROL

More and more today our world seems out of control. We live in a world of cascading crises. Violence is mushrooming. Division is mounting. Global debt is snowballing. The earth itself is groaning as natural disasters are becoming more commonplace and destructive. Seemingly unsolvable problems plague our nation and global community.

Dr. David Jeremiah said it well: "I can understand why people shudder at today's headlines. The daily news shows an alarming disintegration of world order and security. We see growing disorder now and chaos ahead, and we wonder whether God has turned His face away from us."[1]

Then he told this humorous story:

> Some years ago, the late pastor Ray Stedman was scheduled to speak at a conference in England. Each session of the conference began with a song service. One night, the leader led the worshippers in the chorus "Our God Reigns." Stedman glanced at the song sheet, which had been prepared by the church staff. What he saw caused him to smile. Someone, intending to type the title as "Our God Reigns," had actually typed "Our God Resigns."

Jeremiah concluded:

> Let me assure you that our God will never resign. We who trust Him have no reason to fear. As I have read Ezekiel 38–39, the one thing that stands out is the sovereignty of God. He is in control. God orchestrates

> this scenario to demonstrate to His people, Israel, that He is their God and worthy of their trust. Israel has no hope without God, and God will win the battle for the nation. Godless Russia is no match for the King of kings.
>
> The God of Israel is also our God, which means whatever we fear is also no match for the King of kings. When it looks like there is no hope, hope is just waiting for the proper moment to show up. God can be trusted.[2]

Ezekiel 38–39 reveals that God is in control. Over and over in these chapters, God makes it clear that He is in charge. If there's one thing we learn more than anything else from this passage, it's that God is on top of things. God's control is evident to such an extent that the prophet encourages the readers by telling them the end of the story before it even begins.[3] He wrote the script; He assembled the cast; He's making sure the stage is perfectly set for His great prophetic production. He's the Director of the entire drama.

That's not only true of nations and leaders; it's true in all of life. In your life. In my life. God knows the end of the story before it begins. He knew the end of your story and of my story before our lives began. The same God who has the entire world in His hands has your world in His hands. God is in control of your life. And His Son, Jesus, is Lord. He can provide for you and protect you in the daily troubles and turbulence of life.

I like the story of a New Zealand pilot named Owen B. Wilson, who wanted to do something special for his friend's birthday. Wilson offered to take his friend flying in his small two-seat aircraft. They departed on a Sunday afternoon after church and took in the splendor of the landscapes and seascapes that unfolded in a panorama before them. At one point, they crossed a tall mountain, and the engine began to sputter and then died. As the plane began quickly losing altitude, Wilson searched the area below to land but saw nothing but steep mountainside. When it appeared they would fly into a mountain, Wilson's passenger cried out, "Lord, please help us get over that steep ledge!"

They barely skimmed over the ridge and then began to pray for the Lord to show them somewhere to safely land. At the last moment, when all hope seemed lost, they spotted a tiny strip of land almost hidden between two ridges. They glided into the narrow opening, touched down, and bounced to a stop. In unison the men shouted, "Thank You, Lord!"

Looking up, just in front of them, they saw a big twenty-foot sign that said, "Jesus is Lord!"

As it turned out, a Christian retreat center owned the field, which explained the billboard. The owners ran out to meet their unexpected visitors and told them the field was normally filled with livestock, but on this day, the animals were lined along the edge of the field, as if giving them space to land.

Our world today is experiencing some major instability.

The same can be true in our personal lives. We often find ourselves flying into turbulence. Sometimes the engines stall. Things might be so bad we find ourselves bracing for a crash. Circumstances seem hopeless. But whatever the situation we can discover the incredible truth that Jesus is Lord.[4] Our God is in control and in charge.

4. REMAIN HOPEFUL

There are many competing philosophies in the world, but when it all boils down, there are really just two: hope and despair. Without Jesus Christ and His Word, all other philosophies ultimately end in existential gloom.

Max Lucado observed:

> We live in a day of despair. The suicide rate in American has increased 24 percent since 1999. Twenty-four percent! If a disease saw such a spike, we would deem it an epidemic. How do we explain the increase? We've never been more educated. We have tools of technology our parents could not have dreamed of. We are saturated with entertainment and recreation. Yet more people than ever are orchestrating their own deaths. How would this be?
>
> Among the answers must be this: people are dying for lack of hope. Secularism sucks the hope out of society. It reduces the world to a few decades between birth and hearse. Many people believe this

> world is as good as it gets, and let's face it. It's not that good.
>
> But people of the promise have an advantage. . . . They filter life through the promises of God.[5]

That's a great description of those who know Jesus Christ—"People of the promise." God has given His people many precious promises to strengthen us against discouragement and despair. According to one count, there are 7,487 promises in the Bible. The Bible is a book of prophecy, but it's also a book of promises, and often the two are closely related.

One of the greatest prophecies of Scripture that's also a promise comes from Jesus. Nothing is more encouraging and energizing than the promise that Jesus is coming back to take His people to heaven to be with Him.

> Don't let your hearts be troubled. Trust in God, and trust also in me. There is more than enough room in my Father's home. If this were not so, would I have told you that I am going to prepare a place for you? When everything is ready, I will come and get you, so that you will always be with me where I am. (John 14:1–3 NLT)

It's been well said that hope is "oxygen for the soul." That's true. The ultimate hope for this world is the "blessed hope" of the coming of Jesus. He will come to catch away His people to heaven to rescue us from the coming time of tribulation on the earth. Then, after the great Tribulation has run its course, we will return with Jesus to earth, and He will establish His rule and reign over the earth. The earth will be restored to God's original intentions. The world will never find peace through diplomacy and negotiation. Peace will only be achieved when the Prince of Peace splits the sky to return to earth.

The exciting thing about the promise of Jesus's coming is that He can return at any moment. He may not come for ten years, but He could come today. As followers of Jesus, we can get up every morning and say, "Perhaps today." Perhaps today may be the day Jesus comes.

This is our hope. In the end, it's our only hope. I once heard someone say, "Life with Christ is an endless hope, without him a hopeless end." Make sure you have Jesus and are looking forward to an endless hope when He comes.

5. REACH OUT TO OTHERS

When we're surrounded by trouble and filled with fear about the future, we can easily succumb to self-focus and live a self-absorbed life. All our time and energy can be exhausted on ourselves. Further, as we look at what's ahead, we can get too focused on the future and interpreting biblical prophecies that we lose our passion for reaching out to those who have never received the truth of the gospel. We can take our eye off the ball.

In his books and sermons, Vance Havner often cautioned believers not to get so caught up in the details of Bible prophecy that they fail to take their responsibility seriously to win people to Christ. In his book *It Is Time*, Havner wrote:

> I know that some are always studying the meaning of the fourth toe of the right foot of some beast in prophecy and have never used either foot to go and bring men to Christ. I do not know who the 666 is in Revelation but I know the world is sick, sick, sick and the best way to speed the Lord's return is to win more souls for Him.[6]

In all the things we do as we await the coming of Christ, nothing is more important and urgent than spreading the message of the gospel. Jesus can come at any moment, and the multiplying signs indicate His coming could be very soon. Scripture even ties our evangelistic efforts to the coming of Christ. We hasten His coming by reaching the lost (2 Peter 3:9, 12).

By any measure, time is slipping away. We need a sense of urgency to reach people who are lost and to fund the advancement of the gospel in all places, including the chaotic Middle East. We've talked a great deal in this book about the regime that leads Iran, the menacing mullahcracy. They are evil and power-hungry. However, we don't want to confuse the powers in Iran with the people of Iran. We're called to love the people there who are confined in a dark place. I don't want anything in this book to be misinterpreted or misunderstood as malice toward Iranian citizens. God loves the people of Iran. Jesus died for them. We need to pray for them and do all we can to see the light of the gospel pierce the darkness.

According to many sources, the gospel is expanding rapidly in the Middle East, especially Iran. Many believe the church in Iran is currently the fastest-growing segment of the church in the world. [7] As the Iranian people see firsthand the emptiness of Islam and the darkness of the mullah regime, they're turning in droves to the light of the gospel. Iranian Muslims are fleeing to Christ in record numbers. What's happening spiritually in Iran is so significant and revolutionary that it has been called "the Iranian Awakening" and an "explosion." The recent instability and Iran's military defeats have only accelerated this spiritual hunger among the Iranian people.

May the Lord help us continue to pray for the Iranian people, and all those in the Middle East, and for the Christian workers who are laboring there in difficult and dangerous circumstances to bring them the gospel of Jesus Christ. Time may be short.

LIVE LOOKING

Events are unfolding today in the Middle East, Iran, and Israel with lightning speed. Unexpected twists and turns are the new norm. It can seem as if there's no rhyme or reason to it all. But according to God's Word, it's all part of the buildup to the end of days predicted in the Bible.

The storm clouds are gathering. The forecasted Persian Storm is certain.

Jesus can come at any moment.

Make sure you know Him. Make sure He's coming for you.

Seize the opportunities you have before they slip away.

Remain faithful in a world that's increasingly faithless and fearful. Remain faithful to Jesus, to His Word, and to His calling to reach the nations with the gracious gospel of life and peace. Live each day alert, aware, and active.

Jesus is coming. Maybe very soon. Maybe today.

APPENDIX: EZEKIEL 38 AND 39

EZEKIEL 38

And the word of the LORD came to me saying, "Son of man, set your face toward Gog of the land of Magog, the prince of Rosh, Meshech and Tubal, and prophesy against him and say, 'Thus says the Lord GOD, "Behold, I am against you, O Gog, prince of Rosh, Meshech and Tubal. I will turn you about and put hooks into your jaws, and I will bring you out, and all your army, horses and horsemen, all of them splendidly attired, a great company with buckler and shield, all of them wielding swords; Persia, Ethiopia and Put with them, all of them with shield and helmet; Gomer with all its troops; Beth-togarmah from the remote parts of the north with all its troops—many peoples with you.

"Be prepared, and prepare yourself, you and all your companies that are assembled about you, and be a guard for them. After many days you will be summoned; in the latter years you will come into the land that is restored from the sword, whose inhabitants have been gathered from many nations to the mountains of Israel which had been a continual waste; but its people were brought out from the nations, and they are living securely, all of them. You will go up, you will come like a storm; you will be like a cloud covering the land, you and all your troops, and many peoples with you."

'Thus says the Lord God, "It will come about on that day, that thoughts will come into your mind and you will devise an evil plan, and you will say, I will go up against the land of unwalled villages. I will go against those who are at rest, that live securely, all of them living without walls and having no bars or gates, to capture spoil and to seize plunder, to turn your hand against the waste places which are now inhabited, and against the people who are gathered from the nations, who have acquired cattle and goods, who live at the center of the world.' Sheba and Dedan and the merchants of Tarshish with all its villages will say to you, 'Have you come to capture spoil? Have you assembled your company to seize plunder, to carry away silver and gold, to take away cattle and goods, to capture great spoil?'"'

"Therefore prophesy, son of man, and say to Gog, 'Thus says the Lord God, "On that day when My people Israel are living securely, will you not know it? You will come from your place out of the remote parts of the north, you and many peoples with you, all of them riding on horses, a great assembly and a mighty army; and you will come up against My people Israel like a cloud to cover the land. It shall come about in the last days that I will bring you against My land, so that the nations may know Me when I am sanctified through you before their eyes, O Gog."

'Thus says the Lord GOD, "Are you the one of whom I spoke in former days through My servants the prophets of Israel, who prophesied in those days for many years that I would bring you against them? It will come about on that day, when Gog comes against the land of Israel," declares the Lord GOD, "that My fury will mount up in My anger. In My zeal and in My blazing wrath I declare that on that day there will surely be a great earthquake in the land of Israel. The fish of the sea, the birds of the heavens, the beasts of the field, all the creeping things that creep on the earth, and all the men who are on the face of the earth will shake at My presence; the mountains also will be thrown down, the steep pathways will collapse and every wall will fall to the ground. I will call for a sword against him on all My mountains," declares the Lord GOD. "Every man's sword will be against his brother. With pestilence and with blood I will enter into judgment with him; and I will rain on him and on his troops, and on the many peoples who are with him, a torrential rain, with hailstones, fire and brimstone. I will magnify Myself, sanctify Myself, and make Myself known in the sight of many nations; and they will know that I am the LORD."'

EZEKIEL 39

"And you, son of man, prophesy against Gog and say, 'Thus says the Lord GOD, "Behold, I am against you, O

Gog, prince of Rosh, Meshech and Tubal; and I will turn you around, drive you on, take you up from the remotest parts of the north and bring you against the mountains of Israel. I will strike your bow from your left hand and dash down your arrows from your right hand. You will fall on the mountains of Israel, you and all your troops and the peoples who are with you; I will give you as food to every kind of predatory bird and beast of the field. You will fall on the open field; for it is I who have spoken," declares the Lord God. "And I will send fire upon Magog and those who inhabit the coastlands in safety; and they will know that I am the Lord.

"My holy name I will make known in the midst of My people Israel; and I will not let My holy name be profaned anymore. And the nations will know that I am the Lord, the Holy One in Israel. Behold, it is coming and it shall be done," declares the Lord God. "That is the day of which I have spoken.

"Then those who inhabit the cities of Israel will go out and make fires with the weapons and burn them, both shields and bucklers, bows and arrows, war clubs and spears, and for seven years they will make fires of them. They will not take wood from the field or gather firewood from the forests, for they will make fires with the weapons; and they will take the spoil of those who despoiled them and seize the plunder of those who plundered them," declares the Lord God.

"On that day I will give Gog a burial ground there in Israel, the valley of those who pass by east of the sea, and it will block off those who would pass by. So they will bury Gog there with all his horde, and they will call it the valley of Hamon-gog. For seven months the house of Israel will be burying them in order to cleanse the land. Even all the people of the land will bury them; and it will be to their renown on the day that I glorify Myself," declares the Lord GOD. "They will set apart men who will constantly pass through the land, burying those who were passing through, even those left on the surface of the ground, in order to cleanse it. At the end of seven months they will make a search. As those who pass through the land pass through and anyone sees a man's bone, then he will set up a marker by it until the buriers have buried it in the valley of Hamon-gog. And even the name of the city will be Hamonah. So they will cleanse the land."'

"As for you, son of man, thus says the Lord GOD, 'Speak to every kind of bird and to every beast of the field, "Assemble and come, gather from every side to My sacrifice which I am going to sacrifice for you, as a great sacrifice on the mountains of Israel, that you may eat flesh and drink blood. You will eat the flesh of mighty men and drink the blood of the princes of the earth, as though they were rams, lambs, goats and bulls, all of them fatlings of Bashan. So you will eat fat until you are glutted, and drink blood until you are drunk, from My sacrifice which I have sacrificed for you. You will be glutted at My table with horses and charioteers, with mighty men and all the men of war," declares the Lord GOD.

"And I will set My glory among the nations; and all the nations will see My judgment which I have executed and My hand which I have laid on them. And the house of Israel will know that I am the Lord their God from that day onward. The nations will know that the house of Israel went into exile for their iniquity because they acted treacherously against Me, and I hid My face from them; so I gave them into the hand of their adversaries, and all of them fell by the sword. According to their uncleanness and according to their transgressions I dealt with them, and I hid My face from them."'"

Therefore thus says the Lord God, "Now I will restore the fortunes of Jacob and have mercy on the whole house of Israel; and I will be jealous for My holy name. They will forget their disgrace and all their treachery which they perpetrated against Me, when they live securely on their own land with no one to make them afraid. When I bring them back from the peoples and gather them from the lands of their enemies, then I shall be sanctified through them in the sight of the many nations. Then they will know that I am the Lord their God because I made them go into exile among the nations, and then gathered them again to their own land; and I will leave none of them there any longer. I will not hide My face from them any longer, for I will have poured out My Spirit on the house of Israel," declares the Lord God.

ABOUT THE AUTHOR

MARK HITCHCOCK has authored forty books related to Bible prophecy. He has earned ThM and PhD degrees from Dallas Theological Seminary and is a research professor of Bible Exposition there. He lives in Edmond, Oklahoma, with his wife, Cheryl, and serves as Senior Pastor of Faith Bible Church. He and his wife have two married sons and seven grandchildren.

NOTES

AN URGENT NOTE

1. "Live—Iran Says Ready for War After Trump Moots 'Very Strong' Military Options," *Iran International*, January 12, 2026, https://www.iranintl.com/en/liveblog/202601054803.
2. "Iran: Deaths and Injuries Rise amid Authorities' Renewed Cycle of Protest Bloodshed," Amnesty International, January 8, 2026, https://www.amnesty.org/en/latest/news/2026/01/iran-deaths-injuries-authorities-protest-bloodshed/.
3. "January 10, 2026—Iran Protests Spread, Death Toll Mounts amid Internet Blackout," CNN, January 10, 2026, https://www.cnn.com/world/live-news/iran-protests-01–10–26.
4. "Iran Demonstrations Against Regime Continue as Ayatollah, State Media Rail Against 'Terrorist Agents'," CBC News, January 9, 2026, https://www.cbc.ca/news/world/iran-protests-friday-pahlavi-9.7039231.
5. "Live—Iran Says Ready for War."

INTRODUCTION

1. Daniel Byman et al., "Hamas's October 7 Attack:

Visualizing the Data," Center for Strategic & International Studies/CSIS, December 19, 2023, https://www.csis.org/analysis/hamass-october-7-attack-visualizing-data.

2. "Hostilities in the Gaza Strip and Israel—Situation Report," United Nations Office for the Coordination of Humanitarian Affairs (OCHA), January 2025, Geneva: UN OCHA, 2025. https://www.ochaopt.org.
3. "Israel Says Airstrike Killed Hezbollah Chief Hassan Nasrallah in Beirut." Reuters World News, September 27, 2024, https://www.reuters.com/world/middle-east/.
4. "Syria Situation Report: Collapse of Assad Regime and Rebel Advance into Damascus," Institute for the Study of War (ISW), December 2024, https://www.understandingwar.org.
5. "Iran Launches Massive Missile and Drone Attacks on Israel in April and October 2024," Janes.com, October 2024, https://www.janes.com.
6. Andie Parry et al., "Iran Update Special Report, June 14, 2025, Morning Edition," Institute for the Study of War (ISW), June 14, 2025, https://understandingwar.org/research/middle-east/iran-update-special-report-june-14–2025-morning-edition/.
7. Claire Mills and John Curtis, "Israel-Iran 2025: Developments in Iran's Nuclear Programme and Military Action," UK Parliament, June 24, 2025, https://commonslibrary.parliament.uk/research-briefings/cbp-10284/.
8. Tammy Bruce, "Department Press Briefing–June 24, 2025," US Department of State, June 24, 2025, https://www.state.gov/briefings/department-press-briefing-june-24–2025/.

9. David Albright, Sarah Burkhard, and Spencer August Faragasso, "Analysis of IAEA Iran Verification and Monitoring Report—May 2025," Institute for Science and International Security, June 9, 2025, https://isis-online.org/isis-reports/analysis-of-iaea-iran-verification-and-monitoring-report-may-2025/.
10. Francois Murphy, "Damning IAEA Report Spells Out Past Secret Nuclear Activities in Iran," Reuters, May 31, 2025, https://www.reuters.com/world/china/iaea-report-says-iran-had-secret-activities-with-undeclared-nuclear-material-2025–05–31/.
11. David Albright, "Iranian Breakout Timelines Under JCPOA-Type Limits," Institute for Science and International Security, May 6, 2025, https://isis-online.org/isis-reports/iranian-breakout-timelines-under-jcpoa-type-limits.
12. Mills and Curtis, "Israel-Iran 2025."
13. Francesca Chambers, "Netanyahu Says Iran Could Produce a Nuclear Weapon 'In a Very Short Time,'" USA Today, June 13, 2025, https://www.usatoday.com/story/news/world/2025/06/12/netanyahu-iran-nuclear-weapon-strike/84177809007/.
14. Ashwin Raghuraman and Davronbek Mamasoliev, "Iran's Proxy Network Strategy in the Middle East," IAIS Research Nexus 1, no. 4 (2025), https://iais.uz/upload/outputdocument/20–06–2025/Iran%E2%80%99s%20Proxy%20Network%20Strategy%20in%20the%20Middle%20East.pdf.
15. Charles Dyer and Mark Tobey, *Clash of Kingdoms: What the Bible Says About Russia, ISIS, Iran, and the End Times* (Thomas Nelson, 2017), 42–44. Note: Syria's political situation has undergone dramatic changes,

significantly affecting Iran's strategic position there, though Iran continues to seek influence throughout the region.

CHAPTER 1

1. "Qassem Soleimani: US Strike Kills Top Iranian General," BBC News, January 3, 2020, https://www.bbc.com/news/world-middle-east-50979463.
2. Barbara Starr and Ryan Browne, "More Than 100 US Troops Diagnosed with Brain Injuries from IRAN Attack," CNN, February 10, 2020, https://www.cnn.com/2020/02/10/politics/us-troops-brain-injuries-iran-attack/index.html.
3. "Iran Has a Hit List of Former Trump Aides. The U.S. Is Scrambling to Protect Them," *Politico,* October 11, 2024, https://www.politico.com/news/2024/10/11/iran-trump-assassination-plans-00183488.
4. Encyclopaedia Britannica, under "Israel-Hamas War," accessed October 12, 2025, https://www.britannica.com/event/Israel-Hamas-War.
5. "Iran Launches Missile and Drone Attack on Israel," BBC News, April 14, 2024, https://www.bbc.com/news/world-middle-east-68820806.
6. Ali Fathollah-Nejad, "The 12 Days of War That Didn't Ignite the Middle East or the World," *War on the Rocks,* October 8, 2025, https://warontherocks.com/2025/10/the-12-days-of-war-that-didnt-ignite-the-middle-east-or-the-world/.
7. "U.N. Nuclear Watchdog Says Iran Could Enrich Uranium Again in 'a Matter of Months,'" NPR.org, June 29, 2025, https://www.npr.org/2025/06/29/nx-s1–5450282/u-n-nuclear-watchdog-says-iran-could-enrich-uranium-again-in-a-matter-of-months.

8. "What We Know about the Iran-Israel Ceasefire," BBC News, June 24, 2025, https://www.bbc.com/news/articles/czjk3kxr3zno.
9. "Iran Moved 400 kg of Enriched Uranium Before US Strikes, Say Israeli Military Officials," *Organiser,* June 23, 2025, https://organiser.org/2025/06/23/298838/world/iran-moved-400-kg-of-enriched-uranium-before-us-strikes-say-israeli-military-officials/.
10. Paul K. Kerr, "Iran and Nuclear Weapons Production," Congress.gov, June 24, 2025, https://www.congress.gov/crs-product/IF12106.
11. Valerie Lincy and Gary Milhollin, "Iran's Nuclear Timetable: The Weapon Potential," Iran Watch, June 11, 2025, https://www.iranwatch.org/our-publications/articles-reports/irans-nuclear-timetable-weapon-potential.
12. Mills and Curtis, "Israel-Iran 2025."
13. Heather Williams and Joseph S. Bermudez, Jr., "Damage to Iran's Nuclear Program—Can It Rebuild?" CSIS, August 13, 2025, https://www.csis.org/analysis/damage-irans-nuclear-program-can-it-rebuild.
14. "U.N. Nuclear Watchdog Says Iran Could Enrich Uranium Again in 'a Matter of Months,'" National Public Radio, June 29, 2025, https://www.npr.org/2025/06/29/nx-s1–5450282/u-n-nuclear-watchdog-says-iran-could-enrich-uranium-again-in-a-matter-of-months.
15. Suzanne Maloney, "The Path Forward on Iran and Its Proxy Forces," *Brookings*, March 1, 2024, https://www.brookings.edu/articles/the-path-forward-on-iran-and-its-proxy-forces/.
16. "Briefing on the Iranian Attacks on Saudi Oil Facilities," US Department of State, September 18, 2019, https://2017

–2021.state.gov/briefing-on-the-iranian-attacks-on-saudi-oil-facilities/index.html.

17. "Saudi Oil Attacks: Drone Strikes Knock Out Half of Saudi Arabia's Oil Supply," BBC News, September 14, 2019, https://www.bbc.com/news/world-middle-east-49699429.
18. Lojien Ben Gassem and Noor Nugali, "Saudi Arabia's Defense Ministry Displays Iranian Drones, Cruise Missiles Used in Aramco Attacks," Arab News, September 18, 2019, https://www.arabnews.com/node/1556271/saudi-arabia.
19. Heather Williams and Joseph S. Bermudez Jr., "Damage to Iran's Nuclear Program—Can It Rebuild?" Center for Strategic and International Studies, August 13, 2025, https://www.csis.org/analysis/damage-irans-nuclear-program-can-it-rebuild.
20. Mehdi Khalaji, "Apocalyptic Politics: On the Rationality of Iranian Policy," Washington Institute for Near East Policy, https://www.washingtoninstitute.org/policy-analysis/apocalyptic-politics.
21. Michael Doran, "The Theology of Iranian Power," Brookings Institution, February 14, 2022, https://www.brookings.edu/articles/the-theology-of-iranian-power.
22. Ray Takeyh, *Guardians of the Revolution: Iran and the World in the Age of the Ayatollahs* (Oxford University Press, 2009), 210–213.
23. Ali Alfoneh, *Iran Unveiled: How the Revolutionary Guards Is Transforming Iran from Theocracy into Military Dictatorship* (AEI Press, 2013), pp. 95–98.
24. Michael Rubin, "Iran's Apocalyptic Ideology and the Threat to the West," *American Enterprise Institute,*

April 10, 2024, https://www.aei.org/articles/irans-apocalyptic-ideology-and-the-threat-to-the-west.

25. Maya Gebeily and Timour Azhari, "Syrian Rebels Topple Assad Who Flees to Russia in Mideast Shakeup," Reuters, December 8, 2024, https://www.reuters.com/world/middle-east/syria-rebels-celebrate-captured-homs-set-sights-damascus-2024–12–07/.
26. "The Israel-Iran Conflict: Q&A with RAND Experts," RAND.org, June 16, 2025. https://www.rand.org/pubs/commentary/2025/06/the-israel-iran-conflict-qa-with-rand-experts.html.
27. Ellie Geranmayeh, "Israel and Iran on the Brink: Preventing the Next War," EU Institute for Security Studies, October 3, 2025, https://www.iss.europa.eu/publications/briefs/israel-and-iran-brink-preventing-next-war.
28. Adlil Rasheed, "How Imminent Is the Next Israel–Iran War," Institute for Defence Studies and Analyses, September 1, 2025, https://www.idsa.in/publisher/comments/how-imminent-is-the-next-israel-iran-war.
29. Yaakov Amidror, "Israel and Iran on a Collision Course," Jerusalem Institute for Strategy and Security, July 3, 2025, https://jiss.org.il/en/amidror-israel-and-iran-on-a-collision-course.
30. Shane Harris and John Hudson, "A Weakened Iran Could Turn to Assassination and Terrorism to Strike Back," *Washington Post,* June 23, 2025.

CHAPTER 2

1. John McCain, interview on *Meet the Press,* NBC, April 9, 2006.

2. "Khamenei: Israel a 'Cancerous Tumor' That 'Will Undoubtedly Be Uprooted,'" *Times of Israel,* June 4, 2018, https://www.timesofisrael.com/khamenei-israel-a-cancerous-tumor-that-will-undoubtedly-be-uprooted/.
3. "Iran Announces It Will No Longer Abide by Nuclear Deal Restrictions," Reuters, January 5, 2020.
4. Valerie Lincy and Gary Milhollin, "Iran's Nuclear Timetable: The Weapon Potential," Iran Watch, June 11, 2025, https://www.iranwatch.org/our-publications/articles-reports/irans-nuclear-timetable-weapon-potential.
5. *Implementation of the NPT Safeguards Agreement in the Islamic Republic of Iran*, GOV/2003/32 (International Atomic Energy Agency, 2025), https://www.iaea.org/sites/default/files/25/05/gov2025–24.pdf.
6. John Mecklin, ed., "It Is Now 85 Seconds to Midnight," Bulletin of the Atomic Scientists, January 27, 2026, https://thebulletin.org/doomsday-clock/current-time/.
7. Josh Weiner, "North Korea Reportedly Offers to Provide Nuclear Weapons to Iran—A Global Red Line Crossed," *Washington Morning,* June 22, 2025, https://washingtonmorning.com/2025/06/22/north-korea-reportedly-offers-to-provide-nuclear-weapons-to-iran-a-global-red-line-crossed/.
8. Yaakov Amidror, quoted in various analyses of Iran's nuclear ambitions and regional strategy, 2019–2020.
9. Ali Fathollah- Nejad, "The 12 Days of War That Didn't Ignite the Middle East or the World," War on the Rocks, October 8, 2025, https://warontherocks.com/2025/10/the-12-days-of-war-that-didnt-ignite-the-middle-east-or-the-world/.
10. "U.N. Nuclear Watchdog Says Iran Could Enrich

Uranium Again," National Public Radio, June 29, 2025. https://www.npr.org/2025/06/29/nx-s1–5450282/u-n-nuclear-watchdog-says-iran-could-enrich-uranium-again-in-a-matter-of-months.

11. Ayatollah Ali Khamenei, statement on X (formerly Twitter), November 2024.
12. Ayatollah Ali Khamenei, statement following Israeli strikes, June 2025.
13. Jeffery Goldberg, "The Iranian Regime on Israel's Right to Exist," *Atlantic*, March 9, 2015, https://www.theatlantic.com/international/archive/2015/03/Iranian-View-of-Israel/387085/.
14. "Israel Should Be Annihilated, Iranian Official Says," *Jerusalem Post*, August 25, 2015, https://www.jpost.com/Middle-East/Iran/Israel-should-be-annihilated-Iranian-official-says-413212.
15. Ebrahim Raisi, quoted in "Iran's Raisi Hails Hamas Attack as 'Turning Point,'" *Al Jazeera,* October 8, 2023.
16. *NPT Safeguards Agreement with the Islamic Republic of Iran*, GOV/2025/23 (International Atomic Energy Agency, 2025), https://www.iaea.org/sites/default/files/25/05/gov2025–25.pdf.
17. Valerie Lincy and Gary Milhollin, "Iran's Nuclear Timetable: The Weapon Potential," Iran Watch, June 11, 2025, https://www.iranwatch.org/our-publications/articles-reports/irans-nuclear-timetable-weapon-potential.
18. Mills and Curtis, "Israel-Iran 2025."
19. Kelsey Davenport, "Iran's Nuclear Program: Status and Concerns," Arms Control Association, June 2025, https://www.armscontrol.org/factsheets/iranprofile.
20. Michael Starr, "UK Parliamentary October 7 Report:

Largest Loss of UK Life in Middle East Terrorist Attack," Jerusalem Post, March 18, 2025, https://www.jpost.com/diaspora/article-846615.

21. Ben Hubbard and Raja Abdulrahim, "Assad's Fall Reshapes Middle East Power Dynamics," *New York Times,* December 9, 2024.
22. Isabel Kershner and Ronen Bergman, "Israel Strikes Iranian Nuclear Facilities in Risky Gambit," *New York Times,* June 14, 2025.
23. "IAEA Chief: Iran Could Be Enriching Uranium Within Months," Reuters, June 29, 2025, https://www.reuters.com/world/middle-east/iaea-chief-says-iran-could-be-enriching-uranium-within-months-2025–06–29/.
24. "Iran-Israel Ceasefire: Fragile Peace After Nuclear Strikes," *Wall Street Journal,* June 25, 2025.
25. Lela Gilbert, "Iran's Aggression and the Shi'ite Apocalypse," *Jerusalem Post*, August 17, 2019, https://www.jpost.com/Opinion/Irans-aggression-and-the-Shiite-apocalypse-598904.
26. Salman Masalha, "Iran's Messianic War," Middle East Transparent, January 6, 2018, https://middleeasttransparent.com/irans-messianic-war/.
27. "Jack Cohen–The Shi'ite Apocalyptic Vision," August 21, 2019, https://israelseen.com/2019/08/21/jack-cohen-the-shite-apocalyptic-vision/. The following is an excellent summary of the difference between Shia and Sunni Islam: Shi'ism results from the beginning of Islam, when after Mohammed died in 632 he had not named a successor. As a result, his immediate followers decided to elect chief among them Abu Bakr as Caliph, both as spiritual and temporal leader. These became the Sunni Muslims.

However, there were many who thought his successor should be a blood relative, and his only surviving blood relative was his grandson Ali, son of his daughter Fatimah and son-in-law Hussein. His followers became the Shia. After Mohammed's death the Sunni Muslims raised an army and began their series of conquests, including Damascus in 634, Jerusalem in 639, and North Africa in 652. The inevitable Sunni-Shia clash came at Karbala in what is now Iraq in 680 when the Shia army under Ali were defeated by a much larger Sunni army under the Caliph. From then on the Shia were a persecuted heretical minority of Islam that developed its own culture. Although there are several sub-sects of Shia Islam, the majority and that practiced in Iran is what is known as "Twelver" Islam. They believe that after the death of Ali there were ten other Imams, who were his descendants and for the most part were secret. But, the Twelfth Imam is the Mahdi or savior (obviously derived from the Judaic concept of the Messiah that Christianity also adopted) known as the Hidden Imam. The Twelver Shia, i.e., the Iranians and their proxies, believe that at the end of days when the hidden Imam appears there will be an apocalyptic bloody conflict between the Muslim believers (i.e., the Shia) and the infidels, which of course the Shia will win.

28. Masalha, "Iran's Messianic War."
29. Hubbard and Abdulrahim, "Assad's Fall Reshapes Middle East Power Dynamics."

CHAPTER 3

1. The Free Dictionary, under "dire straits," https://www.thefreedictionary.com/dire+straits.

2. Phillip Brown et al., "Iran Conflict and the Strait of Hormuz: Oil and Gas Market Impacts," Congress.gov, https://www.congress.gov/crs-product/R45281.
3. "Iran Tanker Seizure: What Is the Strait of Hormuz?" BBC News, July 29, 2019, https://www.bbc.com/news/world-middle-east-49070882.
4. "Iran Tanker Seizure."
5. Nasser Karimi and Jon Gambrell, "China, Iran and Russia Hold Joint Naval Drills in Mideast," *DefenseNews,* March 11, 2025, https://www.defensenews.com/global/mideast-africa/2025/03/11/china-iran-and-russia-hold-joint-naval-drills-in-mideast/.
6. Ramtin Arablouei and Rund Abdelfatah, "Remembering the 'Tanker War' of the 1980s," NPR, August 1, 2019, https://www.npr.org/2019/08/01/747170673/remembering-the-tanker-war-of-the-1980s.
7. "Iran Launches Missile and Drone Attack on Israel," BBC News, April 14, 2024, https://www.bbc.com/news/world-middle-east-68820806.
8. Ali Fathollah- Nejad, "The 12 Days of War That Didn't Ignite the Middle East or the World," War on the Rocks, October 8, 2025, https://warontherocks.com/2025/10/the-12-days-of-war-that-didnt-ignite-the-middle-east-or-the-world/.
9. "What We Know About the Iran-Israel Ceasefire," BBC News, June 24, 2025, https://www.bbc.com/news/articles/czjk3kxr3zno.
10. "What Is the Strait of Hormuz, Could It Factor Into Israel-Iran Conflict?" Al-Jazeera, June 14, 2025, https://www.aljazeera.com/news/2025/6/14/what-is-the-strait-of-hormuz-could-it-factor-into-israel-iran-conflict.

11. Karimi and Gambrell, "China, Iran and Russia."
12. "Navy Chief Declares Full Readiness of Iranian Armed Forces," Mehr News Agency, January 26, 2026, https://en.mehrnews.com/news/241101/Iran-Navy-chief-vows-full-readiness-to-take-on-enemy.
13. Robin Wright, "Iran's Eye-for-an-Eye Strategy in the Gulf," *New Yorker*, July 19, 2019, https://www.newyorker.com/news/our-columnists/irans-eye-for-an-eye-strategy-in-the-gulf.

CHAPTER 5

1. J. R. R. Tolkien, Gandalf, *The Lord of the Rings: The Return of the King*, The Quotations Page, accessed February 6, 2026, http://www.quotationspage.com/quote/31806.html.
2. Charles Dyer and Mark Tobey, *Clash of Kingdoms: What the Bible Says About Russia, ISIS, Iran, and the End Times* (Thomas Nelson, 2017), 46.
3. Joel C. Rosenberg, "Putin Rising: But Is He "Gog"? *Joel C. Rosenberg's Blog*, August 17, 2011, https://flashtrafficblog.allisrael.com/2011/08/17/putin-rising-but-is-he-gog/.
4. Thomas Grove, "Czar Vladimir? Putin Acolytes Want to Bring Back the Monarchy," *Wall Street Journal*, December 13, 2018, https://www.wsj.com/articles/czar-vladimir-putin-acolytes-want-to-bring-back-the-monarchy-11544732680.
5. Josephus, *Antiquities* 1.6.1.
6. The Hebrew scholar Gesenius identified Rosh as Russia. Gesenius, *Gesenius' Hebrew-Chaldee Lexicon to the Old Testament* (Eerdmans, 1949), 752. For

an excellent presentation of the grammatical and philological support for taking Rosh as a place name, see James D. Price, "Rosh: An Ancient Land Known to Ezekiel," *Grace Theological Journal* 6 (1985): 67–89; Clyde E. Billington, Jr., "The Rosh People in History and Prophecy (Part One)," *Michigan Theological Journal* 3 (1992): 55–64; Clyde E. Billington Jr., "The Rosh People in History and Prophecy (Part Two)" *Michigan Theological Journal* 3 (1992): 143–174; Clyde E. Billington Jr., "The Rosh People in History and Prophecy (Part Three)," *Michigan Theological Journal* 4 (1993): 39–62; Jon Mark Ruthven and Ihab Griess, *The Prophecy That Is Shaping History: New Research on Ezekiel's Vision of the End* (Xulon Press, 2003), 61–62.

7. Katie Sanders, "Did Vladimir Putin Call the Breakup of the USSR 'The Greatest Geopolitical Tragedy of the 20th Century?'," politifact.com, March 6, 2014, https://www.politifact.com/punditfact/statements/2014/mar/06/john-bolton/did-vladimir-putin-call-breakup-ussr-greatest-geop/.
8. Amine Ghoulidid, "Russia's Libya Push Should Alarm the U.S. and Europe," The Heritage Foundation, June 30, 2025, https://www.heritage.org/global-politics/commentary/russias-libya-push-should-alarm-the-us-and-europe-0.
9. Josephus, *Antiquities* 1.6.1. Yamauchi provides a thorough description of the ancient Scythians. Edwin M. Yamauchi, *Foes from the Northern Frontier* (Baker, 1992), 64–109.
10. "Turkey Opposed to Anyone That Stands by Israel, says Erdoğan," *Ahval News*, July 29, 2019, https://

ahvalnews.com/turkey-israel/turkey-opposed-anyone-stands-israel-says-erdogan.

11. Seth Frantzman, "Turkey Eyes More Influence in Iraq, Syria, Gaza After Deal," *The Jerusalem Post*, October 12, 2025, https://www.jpost.com/middle-east/article-870117.
12. Arnold Fruchtenbaum, *The Footsteps of the Messiah: A Study of the Sequence of Prophetic Events*, rev. ed. (Ariel Ministries, 2003), 111–112. A place known as Tarshish was located on the east coast of Africa, although the exact location is not known. Some place Tarshish in England and from this view they argue that the merchants of Tarshish are the colonies and eventually the nations that rose from England. This view is used to identify the United States as the "young lions of Tarshish." I reject this view. It's far too tenuous to use this cryptic phrase to find America in Ezekiel's prophecy.
13. John Phillips, *Exploring the Future: A Comprehensive Guide to Bible Prophecy* (Kregel, 2003), 316.
14. Behnam Ben Taleblu, "The Uncomfortable Reality of Russia and Iran's New Defense Relationship," *War on the Rocks,* July 22, 2024, https://warontherocks.com/2024/07/the-uncomfortable-reality-of-russia-and-irans-new-defense-relationship//; see also "How Iran's drones supercharged Russia's 1,000-day fight in Ukraine," *Iran International,* November 19, 2024, https://www.iranintl.com/en/202411197064.
15. "The Fall of the Assad Regime: Regional and International Power Shifts," *Stiftung Wissenschaft und Politik*, December 2024, https://www.swp-berlin.org/en/publication/the-fall-of-the-assad-regime-regional-and-international-power-shifts.

16. Lazar Berman, "Israel Hit Nuke Weapons Research Site in Iran Last Month, Set Back Program—Report," *The Times of Israel,* November 16, 2024, https://www.timesofisrael.com/israel-targeted-secret-nuclear-weapons-research-in-iran-strikes-last-month-report//. See also "Hezbollah Is Weakened, But Still Dangerous," *The Washington Institute,* accessed October 10, 2025, https://www.washingtoninstitute.org/policy-analysis/hezbollah-weakened-still-dangerous and see "Syria's Assad Resigns and Leaves the Country After Stunning Rebel Blitz, Russia Says," ABC News, December 9, 2024, https://abcnews.go.com/International/syrian-rebels-claimed-4-cities-24-hours-now/story?id=116562929.
17. "Mahdism: The Apocalyptic Ideology Behind Iran's Nuclear Program," *Middle East Forum,* December 21, 2023, https://www.meforum.org/mahdism-the-apocalyptic-ideology-behind-iran. Also see "Real-Time Analysis: Iran After the Israeli Strikes: Regime Change Remains Unlikely but Not Impossible," *New Lines Institute,* June 18, 2025, https://newlinesinstitute.org/strategic-competition/regional-competition/real-time-analysis-iran-after-the-israeli-strikes-regime-change-remains-unlikely-but-not-impossible/.
18. Joel C. Rosenberg, "Putin Rising: But Is He 'Gog'?" *Joel C. Rosenberg's Blog*, August 17, 2011, https://flashtrafficblog, allisrael.com/2011/08/17/putin-rising-but-is-he-gog/.

CHAPTER 6

1. "D-Day Fast Facts," CNN, June 11, 2019, https://www

.cnn.com/2013/06/03/world/europe/d-day-fast-facts /index.html.

2. Walter C. Kaiser, Jr., *Preaching and Teaching the Last Things: Old Testament Eschatology for the Life of the Church* (Baker Academic, 2011), 90.
3. Kaiser, *Preaching and Teaching the Last Things*, 89–90.
4. Joel C. Rosenberg, *Epicenter: Why the Current Rumblings in the Middle East Will Change Your Future* (Tyndale, 2006), 165.
5. Putting this invasion before the rapture is problematic because Ezekiel places the invasion in the "latter years" (Ezekiel 38:8) and "last days" (Ezekiel 38:16) of Israel's history. While the church is still on the earth, God's final program for Israel will still be on hold. The latter years for Israel will begin with the Tribulation period.
6. One reason these two events are equated by some is because they both mention a great bird supper (Ezekiel 39:17–21 and Revelation 19:17–18). The main problem with equating Ezekiel 38 with the Battle of Armageddon is that Ezekiel says the invasion will occur at a time when Israel is "at rest" and "living securely." Armageddon occurs at the end of the Tribulation, which is one time when Israel will be in danger. Placing Ezekiel 38 at the end of the Tribulation fails to meet this chronological marker in Ezekiel 38.
7. The only mention of Gog and Magog outside Ezekiel 38–39 is Revelation 20:8. For this reason, equating these two passages is viewed by many as the simplest solution to the timing of the invasion in Ezekiel 38. However, two points argue against equating these two passages. First, Ezekiel 38 lists specific nations that

will come against Israel, while Revelation 20 refers to all nations. Second, Ezekiel 38–39 occurs before the coming millennium and time of Israel's final restoration while Revelation 20:8 comes after the one-thousand-year reign of Christ on earth described in Revelation 20:1–6. This raises an interesting question. If these are two different battles, separated from each other by more than one thousand years, then why are they both called Gog and Magog? The preferred explanation is that John uses the phrase from the Old Testament in a summary fashion, like we might use the word *Waterloo*. Or John may employ this term in the same way we tie together two great wars involving the same location as World War I and World War II. John's use of "Gog and Magog" signals to anyone familiar with the Old Testament that he's describing an all-out war against God and His people where the invaders are obliterated by supernatural intervention.

8. John F. Walvoord, *The Nations in Prophecy* (Zondervan, 1967), 110.
9. David Jeremiah, *Is This the End?* (Thomas Nelson, 2016), 226.
10. Walvoord, *The Nations in Prophecy*, 110.
11. Walvoord, *The Nations in Prophecy*, 115.
12. Warren W. Wiersbe, *The Wiersbe Bible Commentary: Old Testament* (David C. Cook, 2007), 1334.
13. David Axe, "After Losing 15,000 Vehicles, Some Russian Troops In Ukraine Are Riding Horses," Forbes, February 4, 2025, https://www.forbes.com/sites/davidaxe/2025/02/04/after-losing-15000-vehicles-some-russian-troops-in-ukraine-are-riding-horses/.

14. "Send in the Cavalry. The Russian Army Plans to Formalize Its Use of Horses on the Battlefield in Ukraine, Media Reports," Meduza, October 2, 2025, https:/meduza.io/en/feature/2025/10/02/send-in-the-cavalry.
15. Albert Einstein, "I know not what weapons . . ." Goodreads, accessed February 6, 2026, https://www.goodreads.com/quotes/14977-i-know-not-with-what-weapons-world-war-iii-will.
16. Charles C. Ryrie, *The Ryrie Study Bible* (Moody, 1995), footnote on page 1,326.
17. Christopher J. H. Wright, *The Message of Ezekiel, The Bible Speaks Today*, ed. J. A. Motyer (IVP Academic, 2001), 322.

CHAPTER 7

1. Adrian Rogers, *Unveiling the End Times in Our Time* (B & H, 2004), 142.
2. Charles H. Dyer, *World News and Bible Prophecy* (Tyndale, n.d.), 13.
3. "Top Iran General Says Destroying Israel 'Achievable Goal,'" *Daily Mail*, September 30, 2019, https://www.dailymail.co.uk/news/article-7520939/Top-Iranian-general-says-destroying-Israel-achievable-goal.html.
4. "Antisemitic and Anti-Israeli Attacks Rise Since October 7, 2023," Reuters, October 2, 2025, https://www.reuters.com/world/americas/antisemitic-anti-israeli-attacks-around-world-since-october-7–2023–2025–10–02/.
5. "Antisemitic and anti-Israeli Attacks Rise Since October 7, 2023."

CHAPTER 8

1. Alexander Fraser Tytler, "Tytler's Cycle," In Between Two Worlds, May 18, 2014, https://www.in-between.org.uk/history/tytlers-cycle/.
2. For a more in-depth discussion of the various views, see Mark Hitchcock, *The Late Great United States* (Multnomah Books, 2009).
3. Joel Rosenberg, *Implosion: Can America Recover from Its Economic and Spiritual Challenges in Time?* (Tyndale, 2012), 125.
4. Drew Desilver, "Key Facts About the U.S. National Debt," Pew Research, August 12, 2025, https://www.pewresearch.org/short-reads/2025/08/12/key-facts-about-the-us-national-debt/.
5. Mitchell Nemeth, "18 Facts on the US National Debt That Are Almost Too Hard to Believe," Foundation for Economic Education, September 17, 2019, https://fee.org/articles/18-facts-on-the-us-national-debt-that-are-almost-too-hard-to-believe/.
6. Jeff Kinley, *The End of America? Bible Prophecy and a Country in Crisis* (Harvest House, 2017), 104.
7. Kinley, *The End of America?*, 98.
8. Kinley, *The End of America?*, 104.
9. Julia Manchester, "Analyst Says US Is Most Divided Since Civil War," *The Hill*, October 3, 2018, https://thehill.com/hilltv/what-americas-thinking/409718-analyst-says-the-us-is-the-most-divided-since-the-civl-war.
10. Steve Chapman, "Is America More Politically Polarized than Ever? Not Quite," *Chicago Tribune*, September 21, 2018, https://www.chicagotribune.com/columns/steve-chapman/ct-perspec-chapman-polarized-america-civil-war-0923–20180921-story.html.

11. Aris Folley, "GOP Lawmaker Invokes Possibility of 'Civil War' After House Votes on Trump Impeachment Procedures," *The Hill*, October 31, 2019, https://thehill.com/homenews/house/468419-gop-lawmaker-invokes-civil-war-after-house-votes-on-trump-impeachment.
12. Bill O'Reilly, "The War over Donald Trump," Bill O'Reilly.com, September 26, 2019, https://www.billoreilly.com/b/The-War-Over-Donald-Trump/580335624758333012.html.
13. Eleanor Pringle, "Ray Dalio Says the U.S. Is Headed for Civil War, with Either Side Exerting 'Tests of Power' on Their Rivals, *Fortune*, October 10, 2025, https://fortune.com/2025/10/10/ray-dalio-us-civil-war-tests-of-power/.
14. Jeffrey M. Jones, "Americans Agree Nation Is Divided on Key Values," Gallup, September 23, 2024, https://news.gallup.com/poll/650828/americans-agree-nation-divided-key-values.aspx.
15. Jamie Seidel, "The Second US Civil War," news.com.au, January 6, 2019, https://www.news.com.au/lifestyle/real-life/news-life/the-second-us-civil-war/news-story/ec43b36de5f5f9f11e478a8fc71ea2dc.
16. Seidel, "The Second US Civil War."
17. Kinley, *The End of America?*, 193–97.
18. Kinley, *The End of America?*, 197–99.

CHAPTER 9

1. Dr. David Jeremiah, *The Book of Signs: 31 Undeniable Prophecies of the Apocalypse* (Thomas Nelson, 2019), 42.
2. Jeremiah, *The Book of Signs*, 42–43.
3. Warren W. Wiersbe, *The Wiersbe Bible Commentary: Old Testament* (David C. Cook, 2007), 1332–33.
4. Adapted from Robert J. Morgan, *Worry Less, Live*

More: God's Prescription for a Better Life (Thomas Nelson, 2017), 56–57.

5. Max Lucado, *Unshakable Hope* (Thomas Nelson, 2018), 10.
6. "Quotes by Vance Havner," Grace Quotes, accessed February 6, 2026, https://gracequotes.org/author-quote/vance-havner/.
7. Kyle Davison Bair, "Iran: The World's Fastest-Growing Christian Evangelical Community," Medium, June 4, 2024, https://medium.com/hope-youre-curious/iran-the-worlds-fastest-growing-christian-evangelical-community-9f887bacf13a.